FOREWORD BY H. E. BA

My Life My Story

Tapping Into Your Infinite Power

A COLLABORATIVE WORK WITH

THIRTEEN AMAZING AUTHORS

MICHAEL BART MATHEWS

Email: wecreatebooks@tmeginc.com
Email: wecreatebooks@gmail.com
Direct: 1.708.634.6785
Contributor: Robbie S. Mathews/Cover Design
Contributor: Stephanie Bradley/Editor
Contributor: Project Manager/H. E. Baron Sir Dr. James Dentley III
Contributor: Project Manager/Michael Bart Mathews

Scripture quotations marked as ESV – The Holy Bible/English Standard Version.
Scripture quotations marked KJV – The Holy Bible/King James Version.
Scripture quotations marked NLT – The Holy Bible/New Living Testament.
Scripture quotations marked NKJV – The New King James Version.
Scripture quotations marked NIV – The Holy Bible/New International Version.
Scripture quotations unmarked or summarized/The Holy Bible or other religious content.

WE CREATE BOOKS
WE ARE DRIVEN BY YOUR SUCCESS

The Mathews Entrepreneur Group Inc
We Create Books Division
www.tmeginc.com

1020 Park Dr, Suite 491
Flossmoor, Illinois, 60422 – USA

Contents

Foreword

While we live in a world with overwhelming challenges, the author's stories illuminate a bright walk of hope.

This book, 'My Life My Story' is not an anthology of despair. It is an empowering testimony of faith, hope, belief, and inspiration of fourteen empowering people who did not run from adversity. When the going got rough, they got tough!

Each storyteller shares their unique journey. Some experience the pain from loss. Others experience different struggles, trials, setbacks, and tribulations that have forever shaped their lives, liberty, and pursuit of happiness. Each storyteller shares the determination it took for them to rise above the struggles and prosper.

Within each chapter, each author paves the way for you to learn from their experiences. Each storyteller is Inspired2Speak about their willingness to be open-minded while finding empowering strength from vulnerability.

While walking their journeys, each storyteller discovered how to harness the power of purpose within. Their Limitless potential begins to shine throughout each chapter.

I invite you to look into your souls as you read each chapter from each storyteller. Think about how you face adversity. Breaking News: Adversity is not the end of the road! By facing adversity, there will be seeds of transformation, change, achievement, and success for those who see the universe reaching infinity and beyond.

There is no room to live in a confined box or under the preverbal glass ceiling of shortcomings. FYI: There is no box or glass ceiling in life. If you think it is, it is. If you think it's not, it's not.

Each storyteller will empower you to *Unlock The Blueprint of Intention* along your journey. May *The 5 Frequencies of High Performance* strengthen your mindset.

You are Powered by Your Thoughts!

H.E. Sir Dr. James Dentley III

Founder of JD3TV/ LIMITLESSTV and Inspired2Speak
Text: MYLIFE to 26786 and receive your free gift.

Introduction

"My Life My Story—Tapping Into Your Infinite Power" combines individual chapters written by an empowering team of fourteen extraordinary coauthors.

We invite you to take your rightful seat around our campfire within the pages of this book. As you read each amazing chapter, imagine sitting around the campfire with us. Together, we are seated under the cloak of darkness with the midnight blue sky as our canopy. Take a deep breath and smell the fresh air as we gaze up into the universe and watch the stars twinkling. See the ray of light from the full moon shining down upon our campsite. Listen carefully to the natural sounds of the owl coming from the forest. Tune in as Mother Nature sings songs from the howling winds blowing and whistling throughout the trees while listening from one storyteller to the next share their story.

Smell the smoke from the wood burning in the campfire. Relish the relaxing, warm heat from the wavy motion of the flickering flames above the burning wood. Listen to the snap, crackle, and pop as the sparks fly above the campfire as each coauthor reads their stories.

Picture the face of each coauthor and listen to the sounds of their voices while you read one amazing chapter after another. As each coauthor sips on a warm, fresh-brewed cup of Iaso Tea from Total Life Changes, you eagerly await the next amazing story. As you turn each page, you begin to think about your own story as you start to compare and contrast your past and present because of each author's empowering storytelling abilities.

Ancient civilizations sought out storytellers who used oral and written works of visual art inscribed in stone and written fables (The Fables of Aesop or The Fable of Marcus Aurelius, for example).

The Native American culture is known for its rich oral tradition of telling stories around the campfire. They relied on their verbal language to share their stories with the next generation. The problem is that when the elders die off, their history, customs, rituals, and legends may often die with them if not told or documented (written).

African enslaved people shared their stories through songs, mostly disguised within the lyrics of spirituals and folk tales. This was their way of recording (they were prohibited from reading and writing) their experiences—these stories were retold secretly to pass on their experience.

In the 21st century, we share our stories using oral, visual, digital, and written modalities. As of January 1, 1978, copyright protection lasts for the life of the author, plus an additional seventy years. These stories and this book will be around for decades.

As you read each amazing chapter, each story will resonate with your mind, body, spirit, and soul. Each author comes from a different life-learning experience and background. *"My Life My Story – Tapping Into Your Infinite Power"* shares a group of unified storytellers who collectively paint a picture highlighting their journeys from not just surviving, but the positive mental attitude it took to thrive when faced with trials, tribulations, and adversity. When you change the way you look at things, the things you look at change. Transformation and change are symbols of growth. One cannot afford to allow hurdles, hardships, setbacks, or roadblocks to stop you from reaching the higher level of achievement that is your birthright to manifest. The only way to fail is to quit!

Conclusion:

"My Life My Story - Tapping Into Your Infinite Power" is an anthology for aspiring authors, speakers, coaches, consultants, business owners, entrepreneurs, and people who need a hand-up, not a handout, because winners never quit, and quitters never win! We, the coauthors, like guides on a collective expedition, invite you to explore the infinite

power within yourself. As you navigate this collaborative narrative, our burning desire is that a higher level of inspiration, empowerment, and achievement propel you to embrace the unique experience and journey that makes your story unique and one of a kind.

With shared authenticity, we ask you, our dear readers, to open your mind, body, spirit, and soul and seek a positive, transformational paradigm shift from reading our stories.

Lastly, remember you are not alone. We are here with you.

Our dear readers, as we reach out across the time and space that separates us, remember the person who is a big success is the same person who was a big failure and did not quit when things go wrong, as they sometimes will. You do not fail if you do not quit. Failure is simply discovering what will not work!

Between 1599 and 1601, English playwright William Shakespeare wrote the following soliloquy in his famous play "Hamlet" – *"To Be, or Not To Be."* Four hundred and twenty-four years later, in 2025, yes, that is still the question today, and it will always be the question.

Click the Link Below To Receive Your Free Gift:
https://www.tmeginc.com/specialgift

Michael Bart Mathews

Co-Founder
The Mathews Entrepreneur Group, Inc.
WeCreateBooks Division
Award-Winning Author
International Speaker
JD3TV-Show Host

1

The Courage To Believe

Kellye Davis

"Mrs. String fellow, you need to get to the hospital now." These are words that no mother would ever want to hear. A joyous car ride with my favorite cousin and aunt on a sunny day turned into a day that would change my life forever. I remembered sirens wailing in the distance. I remembered witnesses signaling the arrival of emergency responders who worked frantically to get my 90-pound bloody body out of the car. The impact of the crash resulted in me hitting my head on the roof of the vehicle so hard that my top and bottom teeth went through half of my tongue. Yes, a part of my tongue came off. My parents had no idea it would be months before they would hear their baby girl's voice again.

During what seemed like forever to recover, I remember experiencing extreme frustration. Not only was I being fed by a nutritional pump and unable to eat my favorite foods, but I also couldn't move my mouth. The pain was incredible. To this day, I can still smell the bloody 4x6 gauze that caught the excess saliva from my mouth. No one could understand me other than my parents. As fate would have it, both of my parents have hearing and speech impairments. Sign language was their primary way of communication, and now it was temporarily mine. I also remember how stressful it was as I would struggle to find alternative ways to be understood by everyone else. The frustration of being unable to verbally communicate for months had become overwhelming and somewhat isolating. Imagine being trapped inside your thoughts, unable to express them to others. It was as if I was becoming more and more disconnected from the people I loved. God used this experience to set the stage for what would ultimately become my life assignment.

Growing up, I was always around people who couldn't hear or speak. My mother was given a vaccine as a young girl, which resulted in a vaccine injury. She lost her hearing, and the older she got, her auditory function decreased. My father was born hard deaf. My grandmother had no idea he couldn't hear. She would tell him to do something, and he wouldn't.

Someone said, "Well, maybe the boy can't hear," and the doctor confirmed that. My father was legally deaf. My parents were always involved in programs, sports, social clubs, and events that catered to the hearing impaired. They associated most with those who were just like them. Learning sign language was effortless. It was all I saw. It was my second language.

Unfortunately, misinterpretation of sign language, lack of awareness of communication barriers, the assumption that all deaf people can read lips, and the assumption that deaf individuals aren't intelligent are just some of the challenges I've personally witnessed my parents endure. I am the eldest of three. My role as a child included interpreting in situations where sign language was not readily available. There was no text messaging when I was a kid. I (literally) became the "operator" for all my dad's phone calls. The amount of patience one must have for that task alone is insane. Advocacy was the biggest task. Appointments, public events, and one of my favorites, school meetings, were places where I would have to ensure that my parent's needs were communicated and respected.

Like most girls, we look forward to marrying our night and shining armor, a beautiful home, and eventually starting a family. Well, I got just that. I was married on my 30th birthday to the love of my life, and two years later, we were anticipating the arrival of our baby girl, Savannah. I remember how enjoyable that pregnancy was. Every day, I saw my body blossoming, glowing, and nurturing the little being God entrusted us with. It was very rare that I would be sick. I could eat almost everything, sleep as long as I wanted, and enjoy the extra attention nearly all expecting mothers get. We had one of the most extravagant baby showers one could imagine. It was incredible. Our family and friends also anticipated and expected to meet our sweet baby Lou. Baby Lou is her nickname, named after my mother and my husband's mother's middle name, Louise.

The news declared a winter storm advisory on one cold night in January. The air was bitterly cold, with snowflakes swirling and dancing everywhere. It was a real winter wonderland outside. You guessed it. It was time to have our baby. Our car slid all the way to the same hospital I was in at nine years old. Our little girl was born just a few hours after arriving at the hospital in what I would consider an effortless delivery. I gave her three good pushes, and she was there. Everything about her was so perfect. Seeing one tear fall from my husband's eye warmed my heart the most. Our family was complete.

Savannah was such a joy to our family. She was growing so fast, very active, and loved bouncing in her baby crib. Around the time she turned two years old, it was time for her 24-month exam. Savannah had a great pediatrician who had been in his practice for almost fifty years. He loved seeing Savannah coming to the office because she was adorable. He would hold her during the entire visit, the majority of the time, knowing just how to soothe her when it was time for a shot. Our pediatrician was the greatest. During this visit, he handed me a 24-month milestone piece of paper I don't recall having to fill out in my previous pregnancy. On the sheets were boxes with YES or NO options. These were assessment questions asking if your child can do this or that. After answering about three full pages of the questionnaire, the majority of the boxes I checked were "NO" answers. My answers were cause for concern for the pediatrician, and further testing was recommended.

Experiencing being told that something could be wrong with your child was like shock and awe. There I was again, feeling muted and distant, not knowing the right questions to ask. What does all of this mean? It never crossed my mind that something could be wrong with my child. I didn't see signs of anything. Or could it have been that I didn't know what to look for?

About a year later, after Savannah turned three years old, I could clearly see something was wrong. She was different. My sweet Savannah was not able to communicate like normal three-year-olds. Her behavior was very awkward. She was obsessed with putting things in order or playing with two of the same objects that had to be identical. She would smear her feces from her pull-ups all over the walls if she were not toileted in time. Savannah would not be able to sit and remain still (for any period of time) other than when she was asleep. There were so many foods rejected by my baby girl that I was sure she was malnourished. Besides, Savannah would fall out in severe temper tantrums for no reason, often leaving me feeling helpless and embarrassed, especially in public. What happened to my baby?

The same year Savannah turned three years old, she was seen by a developmental pediatrician. I remember the day as if it were yesterday. It was just her and I. The doctor asked me a million questions as he observed her sitting in the middle of the floor, lining objects up perfectly, not uttering a word. He stated, "Mrs. Davis, Savannah is on the Autism spectrum." He said more, but I heard nothing after that. I was lost in my thoughts, as if I was in another world. I barely registered what he said after the word Autism.

My only question to him was, "Will it go away?" He replied, "Not Quite." At that point, I'd heard enough. With one hand, I scooped my baby girl off the floor and held my purse and the daunting printout of that visit in the other. After securing Savannah in her child seat, I reread the diagnosis on the now wrinkled printout and sobbed. I was again confused about what all this meant.

It was recommended that we have visits every six months to monitor any signs of progress or regression. We were provided additional services such as speech, occupational, and social therapy. These caretakers would come to my home to help Savannah and sometimes leave worn out from chasing her around and trying to keep Savannah engaged while the ladies were trying to keep up with the wigs, work badges, and earrings that Savannah would pull off. They would assure me that they were okay, but that didn't make it all right for me. After they left, it would be just her and I again. I was growing tired. My husband was not as hands-on as I was due to his work schedule. Honestly, his unawareness of Savannah's needs emotionally strained our marriage. I truly believe he didn't do much because he didn't know what to do. I would be so angry with my husband because I felt alone in dealing with our diagnosed "special needs child." Savannah's behavior took a toll on our marriage. Most days, we grew frustrated with our daily tasks with Savannah. We began to grow frustrated with one another. We didn't have many people that we could call on for help besides our mothers. They were very good with Savannah. I truly thank God for them both, but for the most part, it was me and Savannah.

I grew up in a Christian home. My Faith has always been rooted in God. I've had several memorable spiritual encounters that only the True and Living God could give. I'd give thanks every morning and ask God to lead and guide my day. Before I'd end my morning prayer, I'd ask God to "Please allow me to have a good day with Savannah." I'm sure God was a bit tired of me asking for a good day because I sure was tired of asking. I never knew what kind of day Savannah would have. I needed all the energy, patience, and prayer to get through the day. One morning, after giving thanks and asking God for another good day, I heard an audible voice as if someone was in my room with a bullhorn that said, "Stop asking for a good day and ask me to heal her." I was standing in my bedroom doorway, stuck like a deer in headlights, and couldn't move. God, was that you?

I fell to my knees and wept after about what seemed forever for me to get unstuck. I knew if God wanted me to ask for healing, he truly wanted Savannah to be healed. I felt such a magnificent presence, and I couldn't stop crying. "God, heal my daughter from Autism," I cried out. The physical and emotional heaviness of caring for my Savannah seemed as if it had been lifted off me while on the floor. Savannah watched from afar before kneeling by me on the floor, not knowing that her journey to true healing had just begun.

We often lack the courage to ask or believe in the impossible because of what we see with our physical eyes. It is the courage to believe that activates our God-given power to eventually see the manifestation of what we are believing in God for. Unfortunately, many will never experience the manifestation of what they are thinking due to a lack of belief. For some, it is the lack of Faith in God's power and ability to work miracles.

Here I am with a word from God and a revelation that he wants to heal my Savannah. I was so happy! I wanted to tell everyone. I wanted to tell the world. But then I remembered it was the world that had me afraid that my daughter would be with a disability for the rest of her life. It was the world that told me she would always be in a special needs classroom. It was the world that said medicate for behaviors. It was the world that embraced Autism awareness when I wanted to be very unaware! I wanted no part of Autism because God said she would be healed. That's it, that's all. This journey wasn't going to be easy or accepted as the status quo, but with courage in my heart, I decided to believe.

I started strong in my decision to believe simply by rehearsing in my head which became a seed in my heart that my Savannah was healed. I would look at my daughter throughout the day and would thank God for her healing. I remember Savannah having a terrible meltdown. Instead of trying to calm her down like I would normally do, I sat quietly on her bedroom floor and thanked God for her healing. More meltdowns would come, more uncontrollable outbursts, and other behaviors presented themselves, but I continued to thank God and believe. The journey had become more about My Faith and my patience, more than anything. Although I had the courage to believe, I was growing impatient. "Okay, God, it's been a few months, and this kid seemed to have gotten worse." I remember standing in my bathroom saying, "You said," as if God needed a gentle reminder about his word to me. I mean, my Savannah is still doing all the "Autism" things and more. It was evident that instant healing wasn't my story. But when are you going to heal her? How much longer?

Growing up in the Faith, biblical stories of healing were common practice if you were a follower of Jesus. Jesus healed the blind man, Jesus healed the lepers, Jesus healed the woman with the issue of blood, and Jesus healed the paralytic, to name a few. In all of the stories of healing, Faith was required. Many great preachers like Kathryn Kuhlman and Andrew Womack hosted healing meetings worldwide, and the masses came out in Faith and received their healing. The truth is, some required little Faith, and others required greater Faith. Some required actual work before healing could take place. Increasing my Faith would mean countless sermons on healing, faith books on healing, and finding testimonials of others who received healing from Autism. I was determined to defeat Autism. I was all in.

One morning during my prayer time, I received an instruction that required an act of obedience. What was dropped in my spirit was strange, but I heard it loud and clear. I was told to come out of agreement with Autism. Wait, how did I come into agreement with Autism? I thought. I would never agree to have my children experience such a complicated life. How did I agree? After all, this was the diagnosis given to us. Once a doctor gives you a diagnosis, that's what it is, right? That's what I was taught. Having worked as a nurse for 14 years, my training told me the diagnosis was the end all be all. How could I not accept the fact that my daughter had Autism, especially after everyone who knows us knew it? What was I to do with this instruction, and even more, how was I supposed to come out of agreement with it?

The very first act of Faith was to part ways with the diagnosis. I truly respected the physician's findings but had to focus on the results I wanted to experience. I decided never to speak the diagnosis over her or label her as an autistic child. According to God's word, I declared that Savannah was set free from the medical terms and diagnosis. I knew my words had power. Now was the time to be careful of what came out of my mouth. It was time that my mind and mouth aligned with how I would eventually see my daughter. Convincing my husband of this new way of moving forward with Savannah wasn't easy. Eventually, by God's grace, he was on board. We both decided to see her as a normal, healthy child. As time passed, I no longer participated in Autism special events. I got rid of every t-shirt, hat, bag, and button I owned that had anything to do with Autism. I was no longer celebrating or participating in what I decided to defeat. Autism had become a foe in my household, and it would not be tolerated. It had to go!

As time passed, God led me to different people who would pray and agree with me concerning Savannah's healing. The stronger my Faith grew, the bolder I became about professing healing from Autism. My actions greatly encouraged others who believed in healing themselves or a loved one. On the flip side, some thought I was crazy. I was told by a friend to accept the way God created her, and "if" it's His will, He would heal her. Clearly, she didn't know what God's will was. According to 3 John 1:2 Beloved, I pray you to prosper concerning all things and be in good health, as your soul also prosper. God's will is that we all enjoy good health. I had another lady try to convince me that Autism was a "SUPERPOWER." I politely stood my ground with these people and didn't flinch! Over time, I would go gray rock with anyone inquiring about Savannah. No matter how difficult things were, when anyone asked about Savannah, I would keep it short and simple, "she's awesome."

God orchestrated our destiny helpers in such a way that it still blows my mind. Savannah was blessed to have an incredible preschool teacher named Ms. Taroza. A God send she was. Ms. Taroza, believed by Faith, Savannah, would outgrow Autism. She encouraged, prayed, and spoke healing over Savannah as well. Ms. Taroza introduced me to other individuals who would later assist in Savannah's progress. At five years old, we began to see significant improvements. Savannah's vocabulary grew extensively. She began to make eye contact with others, her food preferences increased, and she was able to sit still more than she ever had. Thank You God! Savannah left Ms. Taroza and started a new kindergarten school. Savannah required special education classes with moderate to severe autistic children. Initially, I was terrified that Savannah would regress by being in the same class with children who needed more assistance than she now needed. I trusted the process. I discovered that Savannah's kindergarten teacher, Ms. Kitty, was also a believer! With over forty-five years of teaching special education, Ms. Kitty taught me how to focus on keeping Savannah calm, quickly de-escalate meltdowns, and other useful techniques Savannah would need daily. I could see it all coming together. The six-month follow-up appointments with the developmental pediatrician turned into yearly visits.

I was so encouraged. Savannah was getting better, and others could see it as well. The next act was obedience to diet, and this was one that many parents with special needs children struggle with. God wanted me to focus on changing Savannah's diet and providing her with proper nutritional supplements. At the time of the original diagnosis, I was asked to list the foods Savannah ate daily. The written report stated, "Poor nutritional intake." The pediatrician didn't provide me with any suggestions or solutions for her diet or nutritional needs.

Like most kids, Savannah loved chicken nuggets, fries, muffins, and sugary juices. To get her to eat, I gave her what she wanted. Textures were a major problem. Savannah wouldn't eat mushy, green, crunchy foods or anything made with noodles. Getting Savannah to eat vegetables was extremely hard, almost impossible. I had no idea how unhealthy her diet was until I began to study the "gut-brain relationship." What I discovered would forever change the way I fed my family. We've heard the saying, "Trust your gut." Well, that's correct. Consider the gut, your second brain. Research shows the connection between the gut and the central nervous system is crucial for regulating various bodily functions, including digestion, metabolism, immune function, mood, and behavior. I knew this was true because Savannah did not have regular bowel movements.

Savannah's skin was also affected by her gut health. She developed dark patches on both cheeks that became worse over time. I started giving her a mild daily detox tea to cleanse, a special powdered multivitamin to replenish her, and a kid-friendly gut flora supplement to balance her gut flora. Savannah began to have more regular bowel movements, and her skin was noticeably better. I also eliminated foods that contained harmful dyes, foods high in sugar, and almost all juices from her diet. We found an app we shopped with that scans all harmful ingredients in foods. Savannah enjoys scanning her foods and learning what's healthy and what's not. Not only was this change beneficial for Savannah, but it also benefited the entire household.

The biggest part of the journey had more to do with me, more than anything. At times, I would get so consumed with Savannah being totally set free from Autism that I would forget to praise God for who He was and not just for what He could do. Healing became the focus instead of the focus being on the healer. Once I came to this realization, my focus shifted. God wants us to have a personal relationship with Him, to know Him deeply and intimately. He wants us to trust in His character, in His love, in His sovereignty, and in His faithfulness. God desires us to seek Him first, His kingdom, and righteousness above all else. He wants us to worship and praise Him for who He is, not just for what He can do for us. In doing so, we will experience true joy, peace, and fulfillment in our lives. Lesson learned.

To (literally) see the manifestation of the seed planted in my heart is indescribable. I taught Savannah how to pray and speak healing over herself. Although she didn't understand that she was different from others, I told her she had a unique ability to learn differently, not a disability. My husband also learned prayers that we would say at bedtime for Savannah. Praying as a family became a habit. Autism had no place in our home. Fast forward, Savannah became a high achiever, specifically in math and history. She earned several awards, including the honor roll in the second and third grades. During Savannah's last IEP meeting, all teachers and school specialists agreed that Savannah no longer qualified for special education classes. I wasn't surprised at all. God said it, and it happened. Savannah is currently thriving at a high level and advancing to the fifth grade. She enjoys drawing, gaming, singing, and traveling. We haven't had to see a developmental pediatrician in over five years. Only God can do this.

I encourage anyone who wants to believe in the seemingly impossible to have courage and believe. We must believe and allow God to work out the details. It is our duty as believers to obey the voice of God in the process. I can't imagine how delayed Savannah's healing would have been had I not obeyed. Our courage to believe could be tied to someone else's blessing. Holding on to hope and trusting in the power of Jesus, who heals, will bring healing to manifestation. It may not be easy. Healing may not be instant. It is the journey that ultimately increases our Faith and draws us closer to the one who heals.

In conclusion, God loved me so much that He prepared me (at an early age) for my own tests and trials that would ultimately give me the compassion, patience, and strength to fight for my daughter. He was with me then. And He is with me now, showing us daily that He is real. It is not God's will that we be plagued with sickness or disease. It is God's will that we be in good health and prosper just as our souls prosper. If God said it, that's what it is. Autism defeated!

About The Author

Kellye Davis

Kellye Davis is a multi-talented entrepreneur with a diverse background in nursing, network marketing, and restaurant ownership. With over 15 years of experience in the healthcare industry, Kellye has proven herself to be a dedicated and compassionate (LPN) Licensed Practical Nurse.

In addition to her nursing career, Kellye has built a successful network marketing business, leveraging her passion for health and wellness to help others achieve their personal and financial goals. As a top leader in her company, Kellye has coached many individuals to success, inspiring them to live their best lives through healthy living.

In collaboration with her husband, Kellye is also a co-owner and operator of a popular Jerk Chicken restaurant in the Chicagoland area. Together, they are learning the restaurant business and what it takes to be successful in the industry.

In all of her endeavors, Kellye is driven by her dedication to serving others and making a positive impact in the world. Through her work as a nurse, network marketer, and restaurant owner, she continues to inspire and empower those around her to live their best lives and reach their full potential. Kellye's commitment to excellence, passion for serving others, and entrepreneurial spirit make her remarkable and inspiring.

2

Breaking Free: Discover Your Power Within

Tara Cornette

My name is Tara Cornette. I grew up in a small town about thirty miles north of Atlanta with one sister and one brother. I grew up with parents who instilled family values and hard work from a young age. I was a well-behaved and studious child. I excelled in school, earning top grades and setting ambitious goals for my future. Little did I know that my path would take me on a journey of unexpected twists and turns. A year after my high school graduation, I decided to get married and start a family at a young age. Balancing the responsibilities of marriage and motherhood of three children, I pursued a career in the medical field. I did this for fifteen years, then decided to return to school and get my cosmetology license.

I want to share my story and tell you how I overcame my journey.

In 2009, I worked at a doctor's office as an Office Manager at a pain clinic. Back then, when you took your cosmetology exam at the State Board, you didn't know if you passed or failed until you received your letter in the mail. So, I continued working, thinking I would do hair as soon as I received my hairdresser or hairstylist's license. However, I continued working at the medical facility. I thought I had seen it all. From managing appointments to handling paperwork and so much more, my days were usually filled with routine tasks. However, one fateful day changed everything. I found myself amid a shocking and terrifying situation that would test my courage and resilience like never before. On the day in question, as I sat at my desk towards the back of the building, I heard a loud commotion that sent chills down my spine. The sound of loud voices and people screaming. With police officers storming the building, busting doors off the hinges, and helicopters circling overhead, panic and fear gripped everyone in the clinic.

As the officers pointed guns at us, they led each employee into separate rooms for questioning, and I felt a rush of adrenaline and uncertainty. The once familiar surroundings of the clinic now felt foreign and dangerous as I grappled with the surreal reality of being caught in the crossfire of a potentially dangerous situation. Amidst the chaos and fear, I tried to remain calm and composed, unsure of the outcome of this harrowing ordeal. I met with the officers face-to-face, and they told me that because I was "titled" as Office Manager, they would need to search my home. They asked if that would be possible, but if not, it was okay; we would get a search warrant. Despite the shock and intrusion, I didn't want them to have to get a search warrant and come on another day. I wanted them to see I didn't have anything to hide or have time to hide anything, so we went immediately to my home. I wanted to demonstrate my innocence and transparency. We left, and they took my cell phone so I couldn't call anyone, and they followed me to my house and began the search. They combed through my belongings and took an unmarked ibuprofen bottle because I didn't have it in its proper bottle. They took a photo album of a trip my then-husband and I went on and met one of the owners. I guess they could show that I had an outside work relationship with them.

Days later, the police called me to tell me that I could pick up my photo album and ibuprofen, to which I told them they could throw it away. They said they couldn't do that, so I had to pick them up. I met them at the office. Since we were shut down, I had to meet other people to pick up some office equipment. The officer comes in and hands me the items; about the same time, 20 other officers come in. I told them it was like living it all over again. The officer told me that indictments had been made, and I was one of them. So here I am in 3-inch stilettos and a dress because I was heading to church afterward. Instead, I get put in a holding cell with a stained and torn so-called blanket and a ½ inch thick mat to throw on the sticky, nasty floor with flies around it. I had to stay overnight, and the next day, I went before the judge, who released me on a $10,000 signature bond. We end up in the newspaper and on all the news channels, showcasing allegations and name-bashing along with our mugshots. My mom called me that day to let me know I was on the news, but not to worry because my mugshot was far better looking than my driver's license, LOL.

For years, I fought and fought this case. They charged me with Drug Trafficking Conspiracy, Money Laundering Conspiracy, and Aiding and Abetting. I found myself embroiled in a complex web of accusations and situations that tested my resolve and belief in the fairness of the legal system. Determined to clear my name and set the record straight, I embarked on a quest for truth and justice that would lead me down unexpected paths and confrontations with the authorities.

In the middle of the legal ordeal that tested my resilience and integrity, I found myself pushed to the brink of despair and self-doubt. As accusations and scrutiny threatened to unravel my life, I embarked on a turbulent journey through betrayal, justice, and redemption. As the battle escalated and the allegations mounted, the weight of the stress and fighting began to take a toll on me physically, emotionally, and spiritually. Struggling to make ends meet and facing the relentless pressure of the legal system, I found myself at my breaking point. As my body and spirit wore down to a mere shadow of my former self, I weighed in at ninety-eight pounds.

On Martin Luther King Jr. Day of 2013, I went into an intense and confrontational meeting at the federal building in Atlanta. I met with the US District Attorneys and my Attorney. We began going back and forth, hands slamming on the tables, voices getting louder and louder while shouting at one another. Tempers flared, and anger arose. The meeting descended into a chaotic exchange of accusations and demands.

Overwhelmed by the intensity of the situation, I reached a breaking point after sitting there for an entire day. I threw my hands up and walked out. I remember going to the basement of the building, where I sat and cried with my attorney and told him I couldn't keep going.

In that moment of vulnerability and desperation, I made a fateful decision to cooperate with the US Attorneys in exchange for a plea deal. The offer of withholding information in return for cooperation seemed like a lifeline in a sea of uncertainty and despair. In the aftermath of the plea deal, I was grappling with the devastating consequences of my choices. The weight of guilt, anxiety, and depression bore down on me as I struggled to come to terms with the fallout of my legal ordeal. As I emerged from shame, embarrassment, and guilt, not knowing if I was even going to survive, I asked my husband for a divorce.

A couple of years later, after several trials, in October of 2015, I went before the judge and was sentenced to twelve months and one day in a federal prison in Florida. The judge stated that by giving me the extra one day in a federal case, I would do only 85% of my time. Therefore, I did eight months in a women's federal prison, one month in a halfway house in Atlanta, and one month in home confinement with an ankle monitor. Not to mention, this month, my divorce also becomes final. The fear set in, but there was also a sigh of relief, knowing I finally had an answer.

On November 2nd, 2015, I turned myself in at the women's federal prison in Florida. It was one of the most trying and worst times of my life. I went through many emotional battles. I begged the Good Lord for three months solid to take me out of this world because I was too scared to do it myself. I walked the track daily, crying and praying. I had to wear a uniform. I had to get up every morning at 4 am, get on a bus, and go to work across the street at the men's prison, cleaning the warden's office. I had to stuff my steel-toed shoes with maxi pads because they didn't have any that fit me. If you cried, you had to cry on the tracks or in the showers. You couldn't cry in front of anyone. I missed my kids, I missed my parents, I missed my job, and I missed my life. I couldn't see past the walls. I couldn't see my future ever getting out of prison. I went through an ugly divorce. My now ex-husband, after eighteen years of marriage, wouldn't bring the kids to see me. I just wanted to die. After a few months, he gave in and brought them to see me.

I was only allowed so much time on the phone, so I broke it down to be able to call home every other night. I would do homework over the phone and email. I learned to crochet and sent home gifts. I would cry and vomit every time the kids would leave to go back home. I missed Thanksgiving, Christmas, birthdays, awards, and prom. Mostly, I missed my oldest child's high school graduation. My girls had to have counseling, and my son just shut down. Again, I felt ashamed, embarrassed, and unworthy. One day, I called home, and it seemed all three kids were crying, and it was chaos. That was when I decided this wasn't about me anymore.

I had to change my mindset. I had to change my attitude. I decided I wanted to live, get home to my babies, and help them. I began working out extensively; I would walk and or run 5 miles a day, and I got to where I no longer cried. I read every book on mindset I could find. I began journaling. I took every little dime I made from the little check I received working at the women's camp and put it into my savings. I would cut hair and trade for what I needed from the commissary, such as soap, coffee, etc. I prayed daily.

After getting released, when I arrived at the halfway house in Atlanta, it was worse than the prison. It was co-ed. You had women on one side and men on the other. You shared the lunchroom and computers. I got my job back at the salon and worked every day I was allowed. I continued to work out. I kept to myself and stayed out of the way of others. I was finally able to go home with an ankle monitor for the last 30 days of my sentence.

When I finished with all of it, I had enough money saved to put a down payment on my house and the first month's rent. I worked every day but still managed to work around my kid's schedules. I went to Goodwill or yard sales each week and bought items to finish my home. It can be done, and I am living proof. No matter what your story is, if I can do it, so can you!

This is where I want to share with you how my experience shaped me in ways I never could have imagined. After all these years, I can finally share my story, hoping it will help someone else from initial shock and fear to the eventual sense of gratitude and resilience. Through the journey of betrayal, injustice, redemption, and so much more, this harrowing ordeal taught me valuable lessons about courage, strength, self-compassion, and the fragility of life. I restored my faith, found hope and forgiveness, and learned to love myself again. It is truly the power of the mind.

My journey continues every day. I find a life filled with possibilities, growth, newfound purpose, and self-love. You can't find happiness until you find it in yourself first. What you believe you can or can't do, you are right. It's all in the mindset. I start and end every day with prayer. I choose to wake up knowing I will have a good day, no matter what trials come my way. Journaling can be so beneficial. Sometimes, I will write it all out and throw it in the trash, but it helps me get it out.

The very first thing I had to do was change my mindset. The power of your thoughts, beliefs, and mindset is everything. Your mindset is the foundation of every action you take. Once I decided I wanted to change things, I had to change my way of thinking. Your thoughts become your words. Your words become your actions. Your actions become your habits, your habits become your character, and your character becomes your destiny. I made up my mind that I wanted to live again. I took every course and read every book I could find to make me better mentally, physically, spiritually, and financially.

The second thing I had to do was forgive myself, and it didn't happen overnight. I carried lots of guilt and always thought of what I should have or could have done differently. Forgiving yourself is not a sign of weakness. It's a must for your mental well-being. Accept responsibility for what happened and treat yourself with kindness and compassion.

Make amends and apologize, including apologizing to yourself. Look for ways to learn from the experience. Forgiveness stops the cycle of hurt and pain and brings in peace. I had to seek counseling for a little while because I kept having nightmares and reliving it all. I had to make myself stop reliving it in my head because I would think about it over and over nonstop. Give yourself some grace because we are all human. We all make mistakes!

Next, I had to learn how to love myself and be happy. Happiness is found within. It was a game changer once I figured out how to be happy. I had to start paying attention to my feelings and how things made me feel. Then, I would decide what I needed to do to make things better. I had to learn that what people thought of me was (absolutely) none of my business. I had always heard that saying but never could do it. Daily affirmations became so important to me that I would make notes on index cards and stick them around for me to read constantly. I removed any negative self-talk. Positive thoughts create positive things.

Breathe. I know it sounds silly, but I had to learn to breathe again. Often, I would catch myself holding my breath. A police officer would walk by, and I would be holding my breath. Most of the time, I would not even realize I did it. Why? PTSD – Post Traumatic Stress Disorder? Probably. When I came into that situation, I had to teach myself to breathe in for four seconds, hold, and then release for four seconds. I did this a couple of times back-to-back, and now, when I find myself in those situations, I breathe right on through it.

We've all heard the saying that the company you keep is what you are reflected as. This is so true. When you have someone who is negative around you all the time, you will start becoming more negative. Protect your peace at all costs. Ask yourself, who do you surround yourself with? Are they helping you grow? You are the average of the five people you spend the most time with?

Set boundaries for yourself and others and stick to them. Be firm and clear about what you need. Know your limits. Learn to say no. This has always been one of the hardest things for me to do. I always wanted to help others, but I had to learn that it was ok to say no. "No" can be a complete sentence. You don't have to say anything else behind it.

Exercise and diet are so brutal in life. Eating less junk food and drinking sodas alone can help so much. Get outside and walk. You don't have to do HIIT exercises. You don't have to deprive yourself. Walking 30 minutes a day, several times a week, is so beneficial. Get outdoors and enjoy a few minutes of sunshine every day.

I say all this to say my story is a testament to the transformative power of never giving up. I want to inspire others to embrace change, take risks, and pursue their path to fulfillment and success. Cherish each moment, find the courage to face unexpected challenges with grace and resilience, and embrace the journey of healing and transformation. My journey may have been unpredictable, but it has led me to a place of happiness and fulfillment I could never have imagined.

I'm thankful God gave me grace and mercy. I am a mom of three and a GiGi to two precious grandbabies. I am a business owner and running a nonprofit. I volunteer and put my face back out in the community without fear. Are some days harder than others? Absolutely. But don't give up! Don't give up! Winners Never Quit – Quitters Never Win!

About The Author

Tara Cornette

Tara Cornette was born and raised in the metro Atlanta area, where she has spent most of her life. Growing up, Tara was always passionate about helping others and making a difference in her community. This drive led her to become a mother to three wonderful children and eventually a grandmother to two precious grandchildren.

After working in various industries, Tara found her calling in the beauty industry and pursued her dream of becoming a salon owner. Through hard work and dedication, she built a successful business that has become a staple in the community.

In addition to her work in the beauty industry, Tara founded a nonprofit organization called "Helping Hands for Bartow Kids." This organization aims to support and empower children in need in the Bartow County area, providing them with resources and opportunities to thrive.

Tara's passion for helping others extends beyond her nonprofit work, as she also volunteers for several other organizations in her community. She is dedicated to making a positive impact and helping people grow and develop to reach their full potential.

Recently, Tara has taken her passion for helping others to a new level by becoming a certified speaker with Inspired2Speak with Sir James Dentley. She shares her story and experiences with others through this platform, inspiring and motivating them to overcome challenges and achieve their goals.

Tara Cornette's journey is a testament to the power of perseverance, passion, and the impact one person can have on the community. She continues to make a difference in the lives of others, leaving a legacy of love, compassion, and service.

3

Narcissism: How I Changed The Game

Dr. Rhonda Johnson

I was conceived by a man and a woman who were married. The problem was they were not married to each other. Each had separate households and lots of secrets. A narcissist doesn't care about other people's needs and feelings, even if children are involved. This neglect can warp and torture a child's mind to the point of not wanting to live anymore. It's not physical abuse that leaves the deepest scars. No, bruises heal, but mental and emotional abuse leaves lifelong scars that affect all your relationships – the good ones, the bad ones, and everything in between.

I started receiving this abuse as far back as I can remember. By age three, my mother was breastfeeding me well beyond the usual age. I vividly recall asking to be breastfed, calling out, "Ninny, Ninny!" But my mother would run and hide, thinking seeing her child desperately looking for her was hilarious. I suppose that's where my need for attention from boys developed. Boys who probably didn't even like me, let alone love me.

To make matters worse, she had no problem breaking the bond we had by sending me to a stranger's home to call another man "daddy." Despite this, there were benefits to being breastfed until I was three, like avoiding many diseases and illnesses. Even now, I'm pretty strong and healthy. However, when I was sent to live with my other family, who I'll call the cop and his wife, I learned what frustration was at only three years old.

My entire childhood was a tale of mental and emotional abuse, rituals, and trauma. I was forced to live with these strangers part-time. They threw me a birthday party for my third birthday, and the cop's mother bought me a beautiful antique rocking chair. It was the only thing that made me stop crying when my mother's oldest daughter and niece left the party. I couldn't understand why they were leaving without me. I loved my sister Betty and her children. We all lived in the same house as my mother. Why was I, at three years old, forced to stay with people I didn't know or care to know?

This was just the beginning of the pain I experienced as a child. I received no validation, no support, and plenty of emotional and sometimes physical neglect. I spent all my time trying to be a good child, hoping my parents would love me and validate my existence, but it never happened. They were so self-absorbed they didn't have time for me. At age six, I decided I wanted to work as a model, thinking it would make them see me.

I had the cop, and his wife take me to a modeling agency to get pictures done. I did a commercial and some newspaper ads. I was on my way until my mother found out there was pay involved. She wanted her share of the money, which wasn't a lot. When they wouldn't give her any money, she shut it down. So, I was hired and retired at age six. By then, I had participated in numerous fashion shows and had some professional training, developing a love for modeling. However, there was nowhere and no way to express my love for this craft. When I was ten or eleven, I started a singing group with my nieces, performing for adults and putting on little shows for the family; no one took us seriously.

My siblings constantly teased me for having light skin, nice clothes, and toys the cop had bought me. No one had any idea of the pain I was enduring, not even me. When I was nine, the cop's son, who was supposed to be my brother, always wanted to play with me. He was five,

I was nine, and I was preoccupied with other things, like questioning why I was there. One day, it got physical. I lightly twisted his arm, and he yelled and screamed like I had killed him. When the cop came home and found out, he took off his big, thick leather cop belt and began to beat me with it. He beat my bare legs so hard, but the worst part was that I was not allowed to cry or utter a sound. This happened a few times, and I hated him and his family more than anyone could imagine. I was never treated well. If his wife thought I was enjoying something, it would be taken away. I could only receive toys, and I disliked ballerinas or Barbie dolls.

When I was older, she took away the books I had requested about going away to go to college. I planned to go to USC, but she hid my catalogs and everything. She later sent her son to USC instead. By the time I was fifteen, I'd had enough. I stopped being available for pick-ups, even when they came to get me on the weekends. Not to mention, I had started getting high. I began hanging out with the bad girls in grammar school around sixth, seventh, and eighth grade. We had an hour lunch break at school, and instead of buying food, we would get weed and beer, coming back to school loaded. We were part of why they stopped letting kids out for lunch.

By the time I got to high school, I had calmed down a little and tried to focus on school. However, I was still quite unfocused as I wasn't allowed to participate in activities that would build my social skills. Anything that would enhance my social abilities was stopped immediately, but I still didn't give up. By the time I was sixteen, I competed in the Miss Black Teenage World Pageant. It was one of the highlights of my life. I enjoyed it.

Despite my accomplishments, I was still unhappy at home. My biggest plan was to leave as soon as I was able. Many family members tried to talk me out of it, so I stayed and attended the local college for about a year or two, hoping to become a nurse. However, my brain was already fried, and I couldn't complete the required work. I dropped out of nursing school not once but three times.

I attended a big concert in a large stadium called Fresh Fest. Performers like Houdini, Run DMC, The Fat Boys, and Kurtis Blow were there. My mother said I could only go if I took my little brother, her youngest son, with me. No problem. So, my friend and I each took our little brothers. They had an event called the "Miss Swatch Watch" Dance Contest at the concert. The winner would go backstage, meet all the entertainers, and possibly get a contract. I knew my friend would win if she got on that stage, so I searched the stadium for her. Finally, I gave up and sat back with my brother. Then the lights came on the stage, and there she was!

The contest started, and my friend was doing ballerina leaps while the other girls were shaking and twerking. As expected, she won. After the contest and concert, we went backstage, met the entertainers, took our brothers home, returned to the party, and hung out with some of the performers. This developed into a long-term situation where I traveled all over the country, met people, attended many concerts, and even fell in love with one of the entertainers.

It was the most beautiful romantic time of my life. Inspired by this experience, my friend and I formed a Sugar and Spice rap group. I was Sugar, and she was Spice. We dreamed of moving to New York and becoming big-time rappers. When I was nineteen, we did just that. However, it wasn't as easy as I thought it would be. Without any support or proper advice, we ended up in a homeless shelter despite my friend having $40,000. Living in that shelter was challenging. One day, a young woman walked by us with a plate of mouth-watering food from a restaurant. She noticed us eyeing her food and offered to help us get a job where she worked as a stripper. Initially, we declined, but the shelter food got worse and worse.

Eventually, we auditioned and got hired. Working as a stripper allowed me to buy good food and save up for a floor-model color TV for my dad. This was around the time crack cocaine hit the streets. I met a guy associated with the rapper I knew, and he sold drugs. Out of curiosity and a desire to make money faster, I invested $500 with him in crack. This was a fatal mistake as the guy ran off with my money. Driven by curiosity, I tried using crack myself. This led to a fifteen-year addiction, with my life spiraling further out of control.

After six months in New York, I realized I couldn't handle it and wanted to go home. I called the cop and his wife, asking for a ticket home, but they refused. This rejection felt like a death sentence. My life worsened, and I remained hooked on crack cocaine until 1999. I flushed many dreams down the toilet during those years. Eventually, I met my husband in one of the strip clubs where I worked. He stood by me, using his work insurance to send me to my first rehab facility in the late '80s. We had a rocky marriage due to my addiction, but by 1987, our daughter was born. I tried hard to stop using drugs, but it was a constant struggle. My baby was born with no drugs in her system, just barely. However, my addiction eventually ended my marriage and started affecting my daughter.

There was one time when she woke up hungry, but I was too busy using drugs to get her food. When I finally went to the kitchen, I found her on a chair, having climbed up to get some crackers. My heart was broken. This memory still brings me to tears. Despite my shame, I continued using drugs until my husband left. Shortly after, I met someone else and fell in love again. However, the problem with drugs persisted. One day, my partner told some guys they couldn't sell drugs in front of his buildings, and they shot him. I felt responsible for his death. This tragedy motivated me to try harder to quit using drugs. It was an uphill battle until 1999 when my life changed for the better.

I moved back to Chicago and returned to school while working for a community service agency. Around this time, in 1995, I was also attending massage therapy school. I got my first massage therapist license that year. Yes, I was still using drugs because I didn't stop until 1999, but I was tapering off, albeit slowly. My life was complicated, and I was in and out of rehab. My mother made it sound like everything was my fault and that she was my savior, but she was the cause of why my life took a turn for the worse. I never had any support from anyone. This lack of support explained why my rap career didn't take off - we had no parental guidance or support.

My friend and I eventually separated. She had a much better sense of self than I did, so she left New York, went back to college, and finished her degree. I became a massage therapist, a certified nursing assistant, and, of course, a mom. I tried to do the best I could for my child. By this time, I secured a decent apartment for us, and we stayed there for thirty years before I moved.

In 2004, while getting my car washed, I met someone. As I waited for my car, a young man accused me of breaking their TV in the waiting room. I thought it was the most hilarious thing I had ever heard. He asked, "Did you break our TV?" Despite my initial doubts, I started dating him. He was one of the most gorgeous men I had ever seen. We moved in together shortly afterward and lived together for eight years. Something just wasn't right. I couldn't give him the love he wanted, and he couldn't give me the love I needed, but we stayed together.

From 2004 to 2012, I helped him transition from working at a car wash to getting a union job and receiving training. I helped him make his dreams come true. Then, in 2012, he abruptly left me for someone else. This broke my heart, especially since my niece, who attended my third birthday party, was dying of cancer around the same time. The pain was unbearable, but I did not turn back to drugs. I endured the pain and sought solace in bookstores, buying self-help books like I used to when I was younger.

This is where I began learning about narcissism. As I learned more, so many doors opened in my mind. I started to understand why I experienced so much pain. I realized who my parents (really) were and why they never supported me. I was on the journey of my life, eager to learn everything about it. When my partner left, I was so devastated that I felt homicidal and suicidal. I even felt that God had forsaken me.

The woman he left me for bullied me on Facebook and through phone calls. I was going through so much pain, but I knew that at some point, someone had to pay for it. I didn't know when or how, but I knew somebody had to pay. By 2015, I was researching online when something popped up about going to school to become a laser technician. I had been crying for three years and felt ugly, so I decided to learn about lasers and aesthetics.

I enrolled in a school for aesthetics and became certified in lasers, eventually becoming a licensed medical esthetician. While in esthetician school, the owner called me into his office, as he did with all the students. It was a small school, and he wanted to know everyone. When I told him I used to be a massage therapist, he asked why I had stopped. I explained that massage therapy is like being an athlete - you use your body for a certain number of years and then retire. He looked me dead in the eyes and said, "Excuse me, do you know how much money massage therapists and estheticians make?" I said no. He looked up some information, printed some documents, and handed them to me.

I met him back in his office the following Monday as he requested. He asked, "Did you do the research?" I replied, "Yes, sir, I did." He said, "So tell me, what do you think?" I answered, "Sir, I think I want my massage therapist license back, and I want it right now." He nodded approvingly and said, "Yeah, that's what I'm talking about, okay?"

So, I found myself studying massage therapy while attending esthetic school. It wasn't an ideal combination, but I had only one shot to get my license back. Everything would be fine if I passed the test after being unlicensed for ten years. By the time I graduated from esthetic school, I would be both a massage therapist and an esthetician. I studied intensely and took the test, but I almost passed. That wasn't enough. Faced with two options, I chose to start over and become a licensed clinical massage therapist. Now, I have two careers and am very happy with my progress. However, I was still in pain from narcissistic abuse.

I tried another relationship, but the man turned out to be unreliable. He was a womanizer with a troubled mind, so I ended it and remained alone for a while. During this period, I decided to become celibate. I still longed for the first guy I lived with for eight years and didn't understand our breakup. However, understanding more about narcissistic abuse helped me move on with my life, even if I avoided relationships with men. I learned to be comfortable with myself despite maintaining a marijuana habit.

I had problems with my daughter, too. I wasn't a great mom and was often distracted by my own issues. I tried to make her do the right things because that was the only way I knew, based on my upbringing. I failed to encourage her, always pointing out her mistakes. I learned how to encourage her as she grew older, but she still struggled in school due to my earlier neglect.

Life continued, and I never gave up trying to heal. I realized many of my problems stemmed from having the wrong influences around me. I lacked validation and was surrounded by narcissists among friends and family. It became unbearable. One day, in 2017 or 2018, I received an email from Bill Walsh and the Power Team. I had been receiving these emails for years but rarely read them. This time, I did, and it changed my life.

I decided to attend one of Bill Walsh's meetings at the Sears Tower. The meeting, with a free lunch, was life changing. Finally, I was around people who could support and encourage me. I began attending these meetings regularly, even traveling out of town for them. At one meeting, Dr. James Dentley was speaking, and he brought along several people, including a woman named Fabulous Camille Robb. Camille introduced me to Dr. James Dentley, and Dr. Dentley encouraged me to sign up for a TV show host opportunity. Although the process was challenging, and I struggled with stage fright and self-esteem issues, I persisted. I continued attending meetings, showing up, and seeking support.

Fast forward to today, the year 2024, I still wrestle with some issues. However, I left cocaine behind in 1999 and, more recently, quit marijuana after a 45-year addiction. The support from JD3TV and Dr. James Dentley helped me focus on self-improvement. Now, I am much closer to where I want to be. I am a published author, have a TV show, and enjoy a fulfilling career as a massage therapist and esthetician.

I love helping people and personally growing as a mother, teacher, and coach. I have extensive knowledge from my experiences and have helped many people through coaching.

Despite attending six rehabilitation facilities, I never gave up on myself. Even when I thought others had given up on me, I kept pushing forward. Every day, I wake up thinking about how I can improve myself. Although I still struggle with some things, I have achieved a lot. I have a Doctorate in Divinity. I am a licensed clinical massage therapist, esthetician, author, and great mom. Life can change no matter what your circumstances are. Keeping a positive mindset and living by moral standards can take you far.

I have role models and guides who help me achieve my goals. I strive to show love to others and, most importantly, myself and my family. Today, I have two more anthologies coming out. I am a grandmother and a coach who never gave up on my dreams. I focused on self-improvement and, in turn, improved the lives of others.

Now, I am addicted to helping people understand the deadly nature of narcissistic abuse. It can destroy dreams, self-esteem, and families. Despite everything I've been through, I continue to climb and develop myself. As long as I keep growing, I will continue to reach my goals and be supported by those who believe in me.

In late 2023, the man who broke my heart in 2012 returned. Most people would have advised against letting him back into my life, but I opened the door. It cost me a lot, but I learned more about narcissism and how to navigate relationships with narcissists. I learned to set boundaries, prioritize self-care, and say no when necessary.

My next book will discuss what happens when you choose to reopen that door. I want to help others understand and navigate similar situations. I am a work in progress, and I want people to know that they should never give up on themselves, no matter what. You may have to remove toxic people, places, and things from your life to get on the right track but keep moving forward. Seek guidance from God, and you will find the right path.

That's my message: never give up on yourself, no matter what anyone says. Keep searching, keep stepping, and keep moving. You cannot lose if you stay on the right track.

About The Author

Dr. Rhonda Johnson

Dr. Rhonda Johnson is an inspiring author, licensed clinical massage therapist, and medical esthetician who has transformed personal adversity into a powerful story of resilience and hope. With a background marked by extraordinary challenges, Dr. Johnson has emerged as a beacon of strength and empowerment to those facing similar struggles.

Born into a tumultuous family dynamic, Dr. Johnson endured significant emotional and mental abuse from an early age. Despite these hardships, she discovered a passion for modeling, which was cut short by familial interference. This early experience ignited a lifelong drive to pursue and achieve dreams against all odds.

As a teenager, Dr. Johnson moved to New York with aspirations of making it in the rap industry. The journey was fraught with difficulties, including a prolonged battle with addictions. After a life-changing stint in rehab in 1999, Dr. Johnson returned to Chicago, where a renewed focus on education and career led to her becoming a licensed massage therapist and esthetician.

Today, Dr. Johnson is a successful professional, published author, and TV show host. Through her writing, she shares the profound lessons learned from overcoming obstacles, shedding light on the devastating effects of narcissistic abuse and the path to healing. Her journey is a testament to the power of perseverance, self-improvement, and unwavering faith.

She continues to inspire and support others through her work, aiming to help people understand and navigate the complexities of narcissistic abuse. With a heart dedicated to personal growth and helping others, she believes that no matter how dark the past, the future holds limitless potential for those who dare to dream and never give up.

Dr. Johnson enjoys coaching, spending time with her family, and contributing to family and community service projects in her spare time. She resides in Chicago, where she continues to make a positive impact on everyone she meets.

4

"Living Undefeated As A Champion"

Marlene Trimuel

"The one who follows the crowd will usually go no further than the crowd. Those who walk alone are likely to find themselves in places no one has ever been before." – Albert Einstein.

These words have always resonated deeply with me, for in the ring of life, I often fought battles that no one else could see. As a lone boxer, I learned early on that true champions are not defined by their circumstances, but by their ability to rise above them.

Stepping into the ring alone, with only my inner strength as my coach, I discovered that living as an undefeated champion means forging your own path, embracing every challenge, and turning adversity into victory. Inner strength, my ever-present coach, has guided me through the most intense rounds of my life. This inner coach wasn't just a source of motivation, but a wellspring of resilience, perseverance, and unwavering faith. Inner strength is that quiet yet powerful voice inside that tells you to keep going, when the odds are stacked against you. It's the discipline to stay focused amidst chaos, the courage to face fears head-on, and the wisdom to learn from every setback.

My journey began growing up in Harvey, Illinois, where love and support were abundant with spiritual values that shaped everything I am today. In our home, guided by two loving parents, five energetic brothers, and one dear sister, the essence of education wasn't just encouraged; it was revered as a pathway to enlightenment and empowerment. My early teachings laid the foundation for my lifelong journey of personal and spiritual growth. My father, a great admirer of Muhammad Ali, lived by Ali's powerful words:

> ***"You don't lose if you get knocked down; you lose if you stay down."***

He instilled the importance of resilience and taught me how to get up and fight through adversity. My mother, a paragon of virtue, prepared me for womanhood with grace and wisdom, teaching me to be a Proverbs 31 Virtuous Woman. My grandmother's spiritual guidance was a constant force, ensuring my siblings and I attended church every Sunday. These weekly rituals strengthened our faith and fortified our spirits.

Even as a child, I noticed how God would speak to me and guide me to make wise decisions and be a leading example for others. I enjoyed encouraging my friends and empowering them to fight for their desires. I could see the good in them and felt a deep calling to help them go beyond their limitations. This natural inclination to empower others was a prelude to what God was preparing me for.

I started ballet at age five and immediately found solace and inspiration on stage as a ballerina. Being in front of an audience and inspiring people with my movements became my comfort place. This experience was a prelude to the more significant things God had in store for me later in life. My early childhood life was nothing short of amazing. As a ballerina, I also learned how to tap dance. For my school plays, I had the honor of being the choreographer. I was able to display my acting, dance, and choreography skills. I was also an officer in the student government, a cheerleader, and a straight "A" student. Excelling and empowering others has always been my priority.

In the fifth grade, I faced a formidable opponent: a stuttering problem brought on by the trauma of a harsh teacher. My words felt like punches that couldn't connect. My voice was like a boxer trapped on the ropes. But even then, a spark within me refused to be extinguished. I taught myself to focus and find calm amidst the chaos, and eventually, my stuttering problem receded. It was my first taste of true empowerment, realizing I had the strength within me to overcome obstacles, even without external support.

High school was a series of intense rounds. I was the fighter stepping into the ring repeatedly, participating in various clubs and events. I learned to empower myself, becoming my own coach and pushing myself forward when no one else could. Each victory, no matter how small, built my confidence and reinforced my belief in my ability to overcome.

I joined the speech team in my first year of high school, and my speech coach, seeing something special in me, told me never to forget him. He said my name would be famous one day and in bright lights. My best friend and I competed in dramatic interpretation and consistently took first place. This, too, was a prelude to the more remarkable things God had planned for me, reminding me of Jeremiah 29:11: ***"For I know the plans I have for you," declares the Lord, "plans to prosper you and not to harm you, plans to give you hope and a future."***

My life took a dramatic turn when I was a sophomore in high school; I lost my grandmother, who was my spiritual guidance angel on earth. Her teachings and example of being a devout Christian shaped my early years profoundly. Though her passing was a significant blow, I realized that her presence would always remain as my guiding angel in my heart. Her influence proved invaluable later in my adult years when I needed her spiritual guidance the most.

I continued to pursue ballet until I left for college, each performance was a testament to the inner strength and resilience I had cultivated over the years. Taking the grace and skills I learned as a ballerina with me to college, I competed in the Miss Black Eastern Illinois University Pageant during my first year. I was honored to be named the 1st runner-up. For the talent portion, I displayed my skills from when I competed on the speech team in high school, creating a dramatic interpretation that captivated the audience. Being the 1st runner-up introduced me to the campus, and I quickly became a well-respected freshman.

My leadership skills were recognized early on when I received the Black Student Leadership Award for maintaining the highest GPA among my peers. I also became a committed Delta Sigma Theta Sorority, Inc. member and was pivotal in nominating Gwendolyn Brooks, American Poet & Author, receiving a Doctor of Humane Letters in 1990. These experiences were a testament to God, preparing me for my purpose to reach, teach, and empower women.

I graduated with a Bachelor's in Speech Communications from Eastern Illinois University and received a full scholarship to attend graduate school at the University of Illinois-Springfield. I graduated with a Master of Public Administration because I wanted to be in a career that served as a public servant. My career is an extension of my personal and spiritual values to serve others. I also received my Master of Christian Studies and Master of Urban Ministry. My personal and spiritual journey is reflective of me holistically and where God has positioned me to minister to women.

My life took a beautiful turn when I met and married my college sweetheart, Terrence E. Trimuel, Sr. Our twenty-seven years together have been filled with love, growth, and shared dreams. We're blessed with two incredible adult children, Terrence Jr. and Tamera, who are a constant source of joy and inspiration. My greatest passions are speaking, reading, and writing. My husband and I co-authored a book called ***"Divorce Your Debt,"*** which became an Amazon Best Seller in Christian Spiritual Growth. It became an unexpected success, resonating with readers seeking spiritual growth. The book reflects our commitment to helping others break free from internal barriers. It's a journey from bondage in Spiritual, Emotional, Lifestyle, and Financial Debt (SELF) to a life of liberation and fulfillment.

I felt like I was finally on a winning streak, balancing the joys and challenges of family life. But life has a way of throwing unexpected punches. I was diagnosed with a brain aneurysm, and suddenly, I was in the fight of my life. Navigating the pain of losing my brother to cancer and my father to congestive heart failure in the same year felt like enduring relentless blows. Watching my mother battle cancer and eventually succumbing plunged me into the depths of despair.

Yet, even in these darkest moments, discovering a deeper source of strength and tapping into my infinite power became crucial. During these times, I truly understood the power of resilience and faith. I tapped into an infinite power within me, a strength I had cultivated through years of facing and overcoming adversity. Psalms 144:1 says, ***"God has prepared my hands for war, and my fingers for battle."***

This verse resonated deeply, reinforcing my belief that every challenge prepared me for more incredible victories.

During my healing journey from the brain aneurysm, I had to dig deep to tap into this infinite power and embrace my inner strength. It was a process that required physical recovery and emotional and spiritual fortitude. Here's how I navigated this challenging path:

1. **Acceptance and Faith:** The first step was accepting my condition and having faith that I could overcome it. Acceptance didn't mean giving up; it meant recognizing reality and preparing myself mentally and spiritually for the fight ahead. My faith in God provided the foundation for this acceptance, reminding me that He had a plan for me, even amid adversity.

2. **Positive Visualization:** I began to visualize myself being healed and whole. Every day, I would close my eyes and picture my body repairing itself, the aneurysm shrinking, and my strength returning. This positive Visualization was a powerful tool, helping me to maintain a hopeful outlook and keep my spirits high.

3. **Meditation and Prayer:** Prayer and meditation became my daily rituals. They provided a way to connect deeply with my inner strength and the divine power that I believed was guiding me. Psalms 144:1 became my mantra, a constant reminder that God equipped me for this battle.

4. **Support System:** Leaning on my support system was crucial. My family, friends, and church community provided encouragement, love, and practical help. Knowing I was not alone in this fight gave me additional strength and determination.

5. **Setting Small Goals**: Recovery can be overwhelming, so I set small, achievable goals. Each day, I focused on tiny steps forward, whether walking a few more steps than the day before or completing a simple task. These small victories accumulated, building my confidence, and reinforcing my belief in my ability to heal.

6. **Mindfulness and Self-Compassion:** I practiced mindfulness to stay present and focused, avoiding the pitfalls of anxiety about the future or regrets about the past. I also learned to be kind to myself, understanding that healing is not a linear process and takes time. This self-compassion allowed me to move forward without the burden of self-criticism.

7. **Resilience and Adaptability:** My resilience was tested daily. There were setbacks and moments of doubt, but I adapted my strategies, remained flexible, and kept pushing forward. I viewed each setback as a lesson, an opportunity to adjust my approach and continue my progress.

8. **Gratitude and Positivity:** Maintaining a positive mindset was essential. I practiced gratitude, focusing on the blessings in my life rather than the challenges. This shift in perspective helped me to see the light even in the darkest moments and kept my spirits uplifted.

9. **Purpose and Vision:** Keeping my purpose in mind was a driving force. I knew my calling to empower women and minister to others was more significant than this temporary setback. This vision of helping others gave me a reason to fight, knowing that my healing journey would eventually enable me to fulfill my mission.

My true calling emerged in empowering women to break free from their self-limitations. I naturally gravitated towards listening to their stories, understanding their internal struggles and the barriers that hold them back from embracing their true selves. I heeded God's call to minister to women. I created a platform where women can cultivate a mindset of living undefeated in all areas of their lives. Through this platform, I've witnessed the incredible power of mindset shifts, guiding women to embrace their purpose, unleash their unique gifts, and make a lasting impact on the world.

Living an undefeated and fulfilled life isn't just about personal success; it's about guarding our minds against negative influences that threaten and hinder our personal and spiritual growth. Nurturing a mindset of resilience, faith, and purpose has allowed me to continuously reach, teach, and empower women to cultivate resilience, embrace challenges, learn from them, and emerge as undefeated champions in their pursuit of purpose and joy. This personal and shared empowerment journey shapes my life and purpose daily with a champion's spirit and trust in the power within me to overcome anything life throws my way.

Living as an undefeated champion means more than just surviving life's challenges. It means thriving in the face of adversity, turning pain into power, and emerging stronger from every battle. Our journeys are unique, filled with ups and downs, victories and defeats. Embrace your journey, with all its imperfections, and recognize that every experience shapes who you are.

Inner strength is the foundation of an undefeated champion. Continually cultivate this strength through self-awareness, resilience, positivity, and spiritual connection. It will be your anchor in the storms of life.

Don't shy away from challenges. Face them head-on with courage and determination. Each battle is an opportunity to prove to yourself how strong and capable you are.

Celebrate every victory, no matter how small. These moments of triumph are reminders of your strength and resilience, fueling your motivation to keep pushing forward.

An undefeated champion lifts others up. Use your experiences and strength to support and empower those around you. Together, we are stronger; helping others reinforces our resilience.

In the ring of life, staying true to your values is paramount. Let your values guide your actions and decisions, providing a moral compass that keeps you grounded and focused on what truly matters.

The most important principle of all is never to give up. No matter how often you get knocked down, get back up and keep fighting. Each setback is a setup for a comeback, and your perseverance will lead you to victory.

My journey has shown me that genuine support comes from within. We can navigate even the most challenging fights and emerge victorious by harnessing our inner strength. Living as an undefeated champion means embodying resilience, perseverance, and unwavering faith in oneself. It means facing life's adversities head-on and emerging not just unscathed but stronger, turning every trial into triumph and every struggle into success. By tapping into our infinite power and embracing our inner strength, we can all live as undefeated champions, ready to face whatever life throws at us and come out victorious.

Marlene Trimuel, "The Knockout Queen"

About The Author

Marlene Trimuel

Minister, Women Self-Empowerment Coach, Author, Speaker

Marlene Trimuel, "The Knockout Queen," is a Minister, Women Self-Empowerment Expert, Speaker, and Author. She is committed to leveraging her coaching and ministerial expertise to guide, educate, and empower women in fulfilling their divine purpose.

The discovery of "The Knockout Queen" emerged during Marlene's recovery from a brain aneurysm. This recovery period led her to develop a blueprint aimed at overcoming stress, grief from the loss of her father/brother, and depression from her mother's battle with cancer.

Marlene's journey taught her how to "Get Up & Fight" daily, finding peace amidst trauma. She is known for her mastery in transforming lives through her transformative coaching programs and workshops, encouraging women to confront their internal struggles, discover inner healing, and develop an undefeated mindset, self-confidence, and life mastery.

Her Coach-to-Fight techniques catalyze transformation, particularly effective for women navigating spiritual brokenness, emotional emptiness, a lack of love, unfulfillment, clarity, and a clearer sense of identity. Marlene guides women toward inner peace enhancement, facilitating healing and access to inner wisdom.

As a Self-Empowerment Expert, Marlene equips women with a Blueprint focused on inner peace, self-identity, purpose, and discovering spiritual gifts. This blueprint was inspired by the ***H***ealing ***E***mpowerment ***R***esources Marlene discovered to foster her healing, transformation, and transcendence.

Marlene's book, "Divorce Your Debt," achieved Amazon's Best Seller in Christian Spiritual Growth. It guides women to identify and break free from four key areas of ***SELF*** debt that hinder living undefeated: ***S***piritual, ***E***motional, ***L***ifestyle, and ***F***inancial debt.

Through her transformative journey of resilience, and coach-to-fight techniques, Marlene's story of ***"Living Undefeated,"*** empowers women to transition from despair, embrace their highest calling, and transcend to impact the world through inner transformation.

Marlene has a Master of Public Administration, Master of Christian Studies, and a Master of Urban Ministry.

Certifications:

Christian life Coach, Women Empowerment Coach, Meditation Coach & Facilitator, Spiritual Life Coach, Success & Life Coach, Corporate Trainer, Certified Inspired2Speak Coach, Practitioner of Neuro-Linguistic Programming, Practitioner of TIME Techniques, and Practitioner of Emotional Freedom Techniques.

Marlene is available for speaking engagements:

Email:	sendherpeace@gmail.com
Website:	www.marlenetrimuel.com
Facebook:	https://www.facebook.com/marlene.trimuel
Instagram:	https://www.instagram.com/marlenetrimuel
LinkedIn:	https://www.linkedin.com/in/marlenetrimuel
Twitter:	https://twitter.com/marlenetrimuel
Tik Tok:	https://www.tiktok.com/@marlenetrimuel2

5

Life Is A Mystery To Be Lived
I'm Far from Done
Dr. Patricia Jo Grover

I am no stranger to lemons; bitter lemons have rained down on me most of my life. I'll be completely authentic, not soliciting pity, nor do I feel any shame. It simply sets the stage for the skill sets and mindset I have developed that serve me well in life and business. Hence my "Rise Above" Platform.

You can quote me on this..." No Matter Your Story, You Can Create Your Own Glory." However, I want it known that I give glory to God for my life on this earth and for the gifts and talents he has given me to help myself and others.

My story begins...

My mother was forty-one when I was born. I'm the baby out of eight. My father was her second husband. She had five children with her first husband and three of us with her second. All I will say is that she did her best with what she had and knew.

My father was an alcoholic and controlling on top of being verbally, emotionally, and physically abusive. He wouldn't let my mother get her driver's license. He made her dress frumpily and wear her hair in pin curls or rollers daily. While he was at work, I would take them out and do her hair, trying to make her look pretty. She would sit there and cry. Of course, I didn't understand. I would say, Mommy, did I do a bad job? She would say no, honey, you did a beautiful job, but now we must wash it and put it back up before Daddy gets home.

Most days, when he got home, he would take my mother and me to the store to buy him beer and cigarettes. He would park so he could watch her at all times. She wasn't allowed to lift her head and have a conversation with anyone. I knew it would be a bad night at home if she did.

When I was three years old, my father tried to kill my mother. He had come home drunk again. This time, instead of just beating on her, he strangled her unconscious on the couch. He yelled at me to go to the kitchen drawer and get him a knife so he could slit her throat. My sister (who was sixteen and had gotten married to get out of our house) happened to be at our house doing laundry (I think that is what set him off so bad this time).

She got on the phone and called the police. I ran into the kitchen and held myself against the drawer, trying to keep him from being able to get a knife. My brother, who was twelve, was trying to keep him from going to the kitchen, but my father kicked my brother off of him. He then got to me standing in front of the drawer, picked me up, flung me against the wall, and got the knife. My mother was still lying there unconscious by the time he got back to the couch. While he straddled over her, the police came through the door with guns drawn. He went to jail that time for more than one night.

While he was in jail for a few days, we left Massachusetts and moved to Maine, where we stayed with my aunt and uncle. They were wealthy and had three daughters, whom he put in boarding school because he disliked having children around. At four years old, he beat my bottom so severely that I couldn't even sit on the toilet for a week. My mother worked the 3-11 pm shift. She moved me and my thirteen-year-old brother out when she saw what he had done the following day. We stayed with a friend she worked with until we found a house to rent. Anything that we had brought up from Massachusetts had been in storage.

My mother worked as a nurse at the State Mental Institution. One of the people she had made friends with was a young man going through the Theological Seminary and doing his internship learning how to deal with Psychological Disorders. This gentleman is the one who helped us move into our rented home. He would check in on me and my thirteen-year-old brother from time to time while my mother continued having to work the 3-11 pm shift.

By the time I was halfway through kindergarten, my parents divorced, and my mother purchased her first house. Mother had to have extra income to afford this house, so we became the first Adult Foster Home in the state - taking in patients from the Mental Hospital (if you ever saw the movie, One Flew Over the Cuckoo's Nest). I lived with that in my house 24/7 from kindergarten until I graduated and moved out. I had to help feed, bathe, and medicate them. One patient had to wear a bicycle helmet because he would smash his head against the wall and scream. We only had female patients until I finished third grade, and my brother went off to college.

The Theological Student was now a Pastor at the church we occasionally attended. He was the closest thing that I ever had as a father. Within a few years, he got married. My mother sold the house and bought a larger one in a different town to take in more male and female patients. I found and saw my first dead body at the age of seven and the second at age twelve.

Genetically, I developed early and looked like a woman at age nine, which caused issues of its own, as you can imagine. I ran away from home a couple of times. I tried to stay out and away from my house as much as possible. Why? Because I seemed to easily connect with adults. I had been exposed to so much, even more than most adults had experienced. Outside the house, I got into situations and around people who weren't from the healthiest environments. Add that to the lack of attention and affection from anyone, especially a male; it is a recipe for disaster. I would sneak out of the house after everyone was in bed and return before my mother woke up. She wore hearing aids. Through all of this, I have always been an excellent student. My mother never attended my parent-teacher conferences, plays, or sporting events.

I started Cosmetology School full-time in the summer before my senior year of high school. Then I went to high school from 8-11 am, beauty school from 12-4 pm, and had to work as a waitress from 5-10 pm or 11 pm at a local restaurant. I was part of a program that gave credit for having a job, and my boss had to grade my work performance. They wouldn't give me credit for doing the other schooling. Doing this allowed me to attend beauty school full-time during my summer school vacation. I graduated from beauty school and high school at about the same time.

My first marriage to my best friend's brother was at the age of eighteen. He had an alcohol use disorder and would often black out. He tried to kill me with a baseball bat, so I locked myself in the car, and he broke out all the headlights, taillights, and windows. He went to jail and doesn't remember it. The divorce was quick and easy since the Judge who put him in jail after his second DUI in two days was also the Judge who presided over the divorce.

I decided I needed to get away from everything and everyone I knew. I spent the summer working on an island off the coast of Maine. It was called the Islesboro Inn and was owned (back then) by Kathleen and David Waterman. There, I bartended, waited tables, and did chambermaid work and the hair of guests and staff members. I was also part of the service staff used when we catered for private parties at the Mansions of the Rich & Famous, who owned summer homes on the island. The summer after I left, Waterman's sold it to Kirsty Alley and Parker Stevenson as their seventeen-bedroom summer home.

At the end of that summer, a friend introduced me to someone they wanted me to meet. He ended up being my daughter's father. I left him when I was three months pregnant because I knew I wanted better for myself and my child—making me a single mom at twenty. While I was pregnant, I went to work at a salon and day spa. I wanted to be home with my daughter as much as possible, so I became a representative of

Tupperware, Interior Homes & Gifts, and Amway. I also found a family-owned restaurant that allowed me to let my daughter stay in a playpen while I cooked and waited tables.

Then, my brother came home when my daughter was one. My brother decided to join the Navy after having faced challenges in college. After his stint in the Navy, he lived in San Diego. Because he had been battling with coming out about being gay, he turned to drugs and alcohol. The drug addiction got so bad that he became a male prostitute to cover the cost of his drugs. He also began selling drugs. During that mess, he ended up contracting HIV and moved back home at age thirty. He became the President of the Aids Network and did educational programs in schools. After five years of bad health, he passed away from Lung Cancer as a complication of his HIV.

While he was home and before he passed, I went to work as a licensed cosmetologist at a larger Salon & Day Spa and became assistant manager. It was also a Merle Norman Cosmetic Studio. Then, I trained to become a Registered Massage Practitioner. I also became an educator for Jessica Cosmetics and Matrix Essentials, Inc. I worked at hair shows on stage, behind stage, and going into salons, teaching how to use their products.

At that time, another friend introduced me to my second husband, who was from a military family. He was a true military brat as an only child; he was used to getting everything he wanted and ended up putting me through bankruptcy. Then, I chose to take a night course in business management to try to better my life.

After that, I took the big step and opened my Salon & Day Spa with Tanning. I had six booths and staff. I carried Matrix Haircare, Skincare, and Cosmetics. When I chose to stop doing the education piece outside of my salon, I created my (own) private line and label of Skincare & Cosmetics. My Salon was Royal Touches, and my line was Majesty. After operating my business for a couple of years, I got engaged to a man who loved me and my daughter very much. He was gentle and kind and would give you the shirt off his back, but he was a very simple man. My eight-year-old daughter could read and do math better than he could. He was a more loving man than I had ever been in a relationship with. I couldn't see myself settling down with him, so I ended that relationship.

Then, I ended up having a relationship with a man who had been a client for many years. We got married (my third husband) when my daughter was nine. He ended up being very controlling, manipulative, and mentally abusive. Everything had to be in a specific place, and canned goods had to be lined up and labels facing front. My daughter wasn't good enough for him. I divorced again, and my daughter was now thirteen.

I chose to downsize my salon and cut back my hours so I could get a job with benefits. I also decided to find out who I was and what I wanted from life. I was committed to learning to love myself and not care if any man ever did again. This is when I took several years to learn to know, like, trust, and ultimately love myself. After dismantling the puzzle pieces that made me the woman I had become, I rebuilt myself again. This was when I developed my Philosophy of Life and the first drafts of the prototypes of the tools I use today as part of my proprietary "Conquering Skills Education."

I read many books, attended many seminars, listened to many fantastic speakers, and matured enough to realize that not only paying attention to other people's wisdom but utilizing it and making it part of my life was wisdom itself! To get benefits and take time to reassess my life and goals, I downsized the salon and worked as a manager at an Estee Lauder store. From there, I was recruited to manage a Bath & Body Works store in the same mall. I kept seeing clients as much as possible, though I worked forty to sixty hours per week in management positions.

As a single woman, I purchased my first house and put a small salon inside to supplement my income before switching companies. My mother passed away, leaving me with my blood sister and much older stepsiblings. My mother never dated another man after my father; she gave up on love. The Pastor, again the closest thing to a father, officiated my first three marriages.

I made it to the highest pay scale that Bath & Body Works would pay a store manager in my state, but I wasn't willing to move. So, I started looking at other options and discovered Avon Products, Inc. was looking for a District Sales Manager in the State of Maine. This was a corporate position with a company that offered benefits, such as cars and other bennies. I was immediately hired because of my experience. With the company car and gas card, my salary equaled a $ 65,000-a-year position.

I managed just under 400 women, recruited new representatives, and trained new and existing representatives to have parties, use, sell, and operate all aspects of their businesses. If they were interested in growing their business by learning how to be a leader, I would teach them how to recruit and develop/grow their teams and teach them how to basically be Mini ME's. As a corporate employee, I was responsible for the sales volume of my district, as if it were a box store like Bath & Body. I was also responsible for losses as in Representatives Creating Bad Debt (orders not paid for). I hired a fantastic Administrative Assistant to help with that because I traveled 1000 miles a week for the meetings and training in the area I covered.

Around that time, I had to have vascular surgery to have the veins stripped out of my legs. It is hereditary in my family. Between road and office time, I worked eighty hours a week. I found it very rewarding to help women who were ready and wanted to help make their lives better for themselves and their families. I was able to help several women make money that their husbands didn't realize they were able to make. Their growth enabled them to leave the situations they were in!

Not that I hadn't dated in those nine years; I wasn't bothering to try to commit. I didn't need anyone to make me feel whole. I was only with someone to get what I needed or wanted on a physical level. I traveled a lot with my job, so I put an ad on Match.com, but I was very specific (I still have the original ad). It wasn't that I liked to take moonlit strolls on the beach; my ad consisted of what my man must be, etc.

After much communication, my fourth husband asked me out on Valentine's Day. I said I don't know, maybe I'll make it. I stood him up because you don't go out on Valentine's Day unless you are a couple. On our first date, he learned that I knew who I was. He learned I could drink, and I wasn't easy or a cheap date. On the third date, he proposed, but I said not yet, buddy! But from that point on, we were inseparable. I moved in with him within three months. My daughter & his daughter met and became friends and lived together in my house. He and I bought a house together and sold his place. The girls still live together in my home.

He worked from home for a large corporation. He and I share that we have both always been interested in owning a campground. We discussed purchasing a motorhome and trying to live in it to see how it would be. We considered purchasing several campgrounds before being together, but the timing was wrong. By then, I was getting frustrated with what the upper management, primarily men at that time, was doing with the direction of Avon Products, Inc. So, I chose to leave my job. At that time, we decided to start a company that would do business up and down the eastern part of the United States, and we wanted to be snowbirds.

We purchased a house in Florida. I still had the house the girls were in, and we had our new house together in Maine. We got busy with our plans for the new business. While away, a property manager rented and took care of our four-bedroom house with a pool eight miles from Disney in a Golf Course Community.

We purchased a Honda Goldwing Trike Motorcycle, which we enjoyed riding. We even had a camper that we pulled behind. We enjoyed Florida and Maine riding and camping. We were down to two houses because I sold mine and helped his daughter, who is now our daughter, purchase her first home. Both girls are still living together as sisters in her house now.

The following year, while in Florida for the winter, we had a major motorcycle accident two blocks from our house. We were not helmet wearers. I don't remember getting on the bike, the accident, the ambulance, riding on Life Flight, being in intensive care for a week, or coming home from the hospital. I don't remember about a month of my life.

I had a fractured skull and a brain bleed. The surgeons had to drill into my skull to relieve pressure. The accident blew out my right ear drum, and I had a torn rotator cuff. I'm officially brain damaged. I couldn't smell or taste things for a long time. I looked like I had a stroke, and the right side of my face sagged. I had and still do have neurological damage. My eardrum grew back, but I have constant tinnitus and vertigo. I had to have speech therapy, physical therapy, and occupational therapy. I would have panic attacks just being a passenger in a vehicle, and I never thought I would be able to drive again. Through much therapy and many appointments with doctors and chiropractors, I was able to heal physically. I said that I would get back on the bike when I healed. We both realized life was too short and that we wanted to do something that was on both of our bucket lists.

Doctors told me that I don't remember what happened because my brain shut down its extra circular functions to keep me alive and let the healing process begin. After I healed and could ride again, we picked the bike up from the repair shop and went for a short ride. We rode to lunch at one of our favorite places, and believe it or not, there was a meeting (going on) for all the KOA's in the State of Florida. We took that as a positive sign and decided to purchase a campground. We did a lot of research, looked at a parcel of land, and bought it. When we owned and sold it, we doubled the business and received KOA's highest awards in all but one year.

Also, at that time, my daughter, our youngest, had a son who, at six months, was diagnosed with JMML, a rare form of Leukemia. He had to have a bone marrow transplant at six months old. (Only fifty cases a year in the US, All Children's Hospital in St. Petersburg, he was the third case they had, and as far as we know, the only survivor they have had). We sold our Florida house after our grandson was diagnosed and started living full-time in our forty-foot Class A Motorhome so we could be as close to them and the hospital as possible.

Our other daughter was expecting twins on Thanksgiving that year. She had the boys fourteen weeks early, over three months early. The big boy was eleven pounds, three ounces, and the little guy was eleven pounds, five ounces (The size of a soda can). The big boy was with us for twenty days before he passed away. The little guy had to have heart surgery and had a brain hemorrhage while still in the NICU. He has also been diagnosed with a form of Cerebral Palsy. We were blessed that we still had both boys with us. It was meant for me to still be here for them.

Then, an alarming scandal hit the news. The Pastor, who had been the closest thing I ever had to being a father, had spent time with my brother and me, while my mom worked the 3-11 pm shift. He was alone with my brother after I went to bed. The Pastor was a Pedophile who liked boys—over the years, supplied them with gifts, toys, candy, and alcohol. Within a week after the scandal aired, he jumped off a bridge and committed suicide.

When we decided to sell our KOA Franchise, it was because we had conquered that goal. We had been there and done that. We were ready to move on to the next chapter of our lives. That was to slow down and finally enjoy the fruits of our labor. Being grandparents, neither of us had gotten to spend as much time as we wanted with our children. We sold our park on August 9th, 2017. At the end of October, I drove the camper van to Orlando to attend a writer's conference because I was finally going to take the time to write my first book.

My husband stayed behind to help the new owners close for the end of their first season, then drove the forty-foot Class A camper down to Florida. He arrived a week after I started writing my first book, but he didn't feel well. So, I immediately went to the doctor with him, and he was diagnosed with Mantle Cell Lymphoma and was given a two to five-year life sentence. We immediately got him into a Clinical Trial at MD Anderson in Houston, TX. When we arrived and secured the motor home into an RV Park, they immediately admitted him for treatment. He was there for months, undergoing treatment. At that time, he would only allow me to tell our daughters. He didn't want anyone else to know. I was in an RV park with our dog, having just met another wife whose husband had recently been released from the hospital. They were staying in the RV park. Thank goodness there was a shuttle to take me back and forth.

I wrote my first book through a Hybrid Publishing Company during this time. They charged me a lot of money. They are the ones who set up my Barnes & Noble and Books-A-Million, as well as my Amazon accounts, so they weren't even in my name. I had 100 copies printed and sent to me for back-of-the-room sales. When I received them, the Hybrid Publishing Company closed its doors and went out of business. I couldn't access any of my accounts. I had to get a new ISBN #, rewrite my book, and go through Amazon.

Once we got him through the treatments and got him to the point that we could be away from the hospital, we moved back to Maine. We purchased a 25+ acre piece of property with a home and put in an 18-hole disc Golf Course and Pro-shop. Because we didn't know how much longer he would be able to keep his job, he wanted something he would enjoy doing outside in nature. Then Covid hit, and it wasn't safe for him to travel back and forth to Texas for treatment. So, we had to get approval for all of the testing to be done locally for his monitoring for the Clinical Trial. We rallied through, his health got better, and we got him into remission.

Once back in Maine, I returned to developing my platform, writing, speaking, and coaching. I learned many things the hard way by being taken advantage of. I trusted some people that I shouldn't have. We wasted a lot of time and money. I started the first version of my show by doing FB Lives or just short video clips. My show began to evolve into a show that was getting streamed and picked up by my local cable TV network. And then I took it to JD3TV Network. I was speaking on more platforms, writing more books (of my own), and asked to submit chapters to other collaboration book projects.

We were going along, trying to live our life to its fullest potential, when he became ill and had to go into the hospital during COVID protocol. Within two days, he was fully paralyzed. On day three, he lost his eyesight. On day four, he had a seizure and went into a coma. I hadn't been able to see him since dropping him off there. After ten days, they couldn't figure out what was wrong with him and had to life-flight him to Boston.

So, I went by myself and was able to be in the room with him every day while he was still in a coma. They had to redo all the tests and still could not figure out what was wrong with him—all these Harvard Trained Medical Professionals. After a week, they told me that they were going to have to put him on full life support. That is when I had to keep my promise that we both made to each other... neither would ever want to be kept alive by machines. So, I had to choose to pull the plug. I wouldn't wish that upon anyone.

Still not knowing what it was that had taken him from me, I made the hospital do an autopsy, and it came back as Encephalitis. At this point, the test results from the hospital haven't come back yet. When they did, the hospital had to contact the National Center for Disease Control because it was the extremely rare Powassan Virus that had taken him. There were no signs of cancer.

Right after his passing, I had to go to the tenant renting one of our houses and give them notice that I would have to sell because I couldn't keep both properties. That didn't go over so well with them. They did approximately twenty thousand dollars in damage to the house, and I had to go through the eviction process to remove them. Also, during this time (three months directly after his death), my stepdaughter went into the hospital. She was very ill, and there was a period when we didn't know if she would make it. I had my nine-year-old grandson, who has Cerebral Palsy, living with me as I was his Power of Attorney. I had to drive him to school, a thirty-minute trip each way, and pick him up after school. Two hours of travel per day. She was in the hospital for about a month before she was able to go home. I wasn't sure for quite some time if I would end up with custody of this grandson.

From the time my husband had gone into the hospital, I stopped being able to work. Our Disc Golf business started to struggle because he was no longer here to tend to it, and I had far too much on my plate. I ended up closing that business and donating some things. I also purchased a new home and sold the place that we had. Then, I returned to Maine to make our final resting place. It was just too much maintenance and too many memories to handle. I took a year off trying to pick up the pieces of my life and put myself back together. I started getting back to work and found it was far too difficult for me to stay at that property. Then, I had to choose to leave that home and everything behind to begin a new life.

I found and moved into my beautiful new house. I decided to finish my dissertation to receive my PhD in Entreprenology. I decided I would entirely focus on my career and the development of my platform. This included writing more books, contributing to collaboration book projects, and speaking on more shows. I decided to Level Up My Show and Speaking Skills while investing in my back office behind the scenes. My back office needs to be in place as my business goes to the Next Level and BEYOND as I am "The Goal Achievement Strategist" and "The Queen of Re-Taking, Re-Shaping, and Re-Making Lives, Businesses, and Futures." I am bringing my proprietary "Conquering Skills Education" to the World from stages all over the Globe, teaching people how to Live Their Dreams Purposefully, Joyfully, and Gratefully.

About The Author

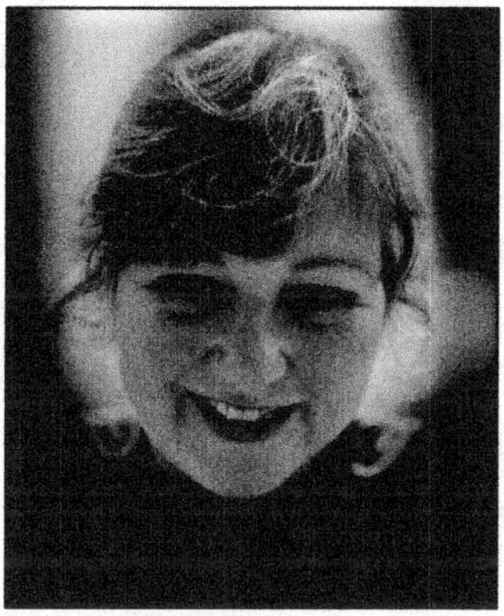

Dr. Patricia Jo Grover

Dr. Patricia Jo Grover, The Goal Achievement Strategist. The Queen of Re-Taking – Re-Shaping & Re-Making Lives, Businesses, and Futures incites action with the platform that she specifically created around her proprietary "Conquering Skills Education" to Engage, Encourage, Educate, Empower, and help individuals to Evolve. Hence, they are able to Elevate and achieve more success as they "Rise Above" any Challenges they may have in any of the 8 Dimensions of Life.

Dr. Grover is a Life / Success / Mental Health Coach with a PhD in Entreprenology. She is an International Best-Selling Author, Global Keynote Speaker, TV Show Host & Producer, Philanthropist, and the Executive Director of her non-profit.

She uses a heart-centered approach that focuses on helping her clients have Mindset Shifts, create New Belief Windows, Raise Their Vibrations, Become Masters of Their Time, Become Extremely Organized, and find their Why & Purpose. Dr. Grover's approach allows her clients to Dream, Conquer Fears, and Create a Work/Life Balance so they can Have, Be, Do, and Earn more while they live their lives Purposefully, Joyfully, and Gratefully. Dr. Grover believes that Success is A Lifestyle and teaches people how to Live Their Lives to Their Fullest Potential.

In her 35 years of Business Management & Ownership, she has recruited, trained, coached, consulted, taught, and mentored over 3500 Entrepreneurs, Corporate Employees, and Staff of her own businesses. She is a Success Sculptor and a Sr. Member of Two High-Level Masterminds and facilitates one of her own. The International University of Entreprenology believes so much in what she is doing with her platform that they have chosen to sponsor "The Rise Above Show" with Patricia Jo Grover on the JD3TV Network and all her events.

6

Timeless Odyssey
Eight Decades Of Life And Wisdom
Dr. Janice Hooker-Fortman

I was born on December 5, 1941, in Dallas, Texas, two days before Pearl Harbor. My father and mother were divorced by the time I was two years old. The earliest memory I have is when I was two years old. My mother had left the house, and I pushed the door closed. When she returned, she couldn't get in and kept telling me to turn the knob. I was crying either because I didn't know how to unlock the door, or because I was scared. But I remember that after she finally got in, she said, "You are going to learn how to read, talk, listen, and follow directions." When I was five and started school, I could read, write, listen, and follow directions! It's funny the things you remember.

I grew up in what was known as low-income housing with my mom, her new husband, and three younger brothers. The community was named Altgeld Gardens, built for returning veterans of WWII, 99% African American, and located on the outskirts of Chicago, Illinois. It was a relatively small community where I went to George Washington Carver Elementary and High School. In high school, I was a part of a singing group called "The Sweet Tones," and I aspired to be a professional singer. Mom had other ideas. "You are going to college, get a degree, and definitely not going to Hollywood!" However, I did not take college seriously; I always partied and played cards in the cafeteria instead of studying. I soon dropped out because of low grades.

I do not remember the 1940s, but I do remember the 1950s. What I remember (mostly) was the gender roles. Men were generally the breadwinners, and women were expected to be homemakers. Racial segregation was legally enforced in many parts of the United States. However, even though it wasn't legal in Illinois, it was enforced in various insidious ways. Growing up in the 50s meant going to school and getting good grades so that you could graduate from high school or college and get a "good government job," which I did. I worked at the United States Post Office and hated it! In the 1960s, there was a dramatic change in our society. Things began to change for African Americans and especially for women. The Civil Rights Movement and the Women's Liberation Movement impacted my thoughts about who I could be and where my place could be. Plus, I watched my mother, a very independent, forward-thinking woman, so I quit the Post Office and started looking for another job.

The employment search where I thought I could make an impact on the mental health of women ended with a job at a mental health clinic for women called the Stone-Brandel Clinic. One of the founders, W. Clement Stone, was a well-known millionaire and philanthropist whom I had the pleasure of meeting. When he would come into the clinic, he demanded us to shout, "I feel happy, I feel healthy, I feel ter-r-ific!" Working in his clinic was a very enlightening experience because I found out that there were so many women, especially Black women, who were suffering from various mental challenges and illnesses. Many challenges stemmed from being unappreciated and undervalued in the workplace and their personal relationships. I didn't realize their situation mimicked mine, especially in the workplace.

I worked in a two-girl office and was responsible for transcribing the notes of psychiatrists, psychologists, and psychiatric social workers. I also had to greet the clients and make them feel welcome and comfortable by doing an intake questionnaire. I often stayed late, conversing with some of the clients, and offered any revelations I discovered. My work was frequently praised. However, my raises were minuscule because of "budget restraints." One night, after all the clients left, it was time for me to lock up. I noticed my supervisor, who hired me, left her office door unlocked, and the keys to her filing cabinet were left on top of her desk. My curiosity got the best of me, and I viewed my personnel file. Job Description: "Janice is a very nice-looking intelligent Negro girl, with excellent diction, dresses appropriately, and has a good personality; although she doesn't have a college degree, she would make an excellent employee."

I looked at the personnel file of the young lady they just hired. She was described as a "beautiful blond" who would make a great asset to the staff. But the shocker was that she had less experience than me and was making $10,000 more a year than me. To make matters worse, I was in the process of training her. Talk about being undervalued, unappreciated, and being taken advantage of! This was not for me, so I wrote a scathing letter to the clinic's administrator, referenced my supervisor and the unfairness of my situation, and quit. I met my first husband after finding another job and joining the dating scene. At the age of 25, I became a wife but didn't become the mom of my wonderful son until the age of 34. Unfortunately, the marriage did not work out. He was extremely controlling, and there was a point when I decided that it wasn't for me, filed for a divorce, and began the journey of a single mom raising a son.

In the 1970s, Black Power was the theme, and I became more "liberated" and more "vocal" about who I wanted to be. I wore a huge Afro, refused to be undervalued and underappreciated, and involved myself in activism and advocacy. "I was being transformed"! I felt my calling was to be an educator, not an office worker. I decided to go back to college, earned a bachelor's and master's degree, and chose the career of being a teacher in the inner city of the Chicago Public School system. I taught Special Education and Fine Arts in elementary and high schools for twenty years. One day, my principal asked for someone to attend a workshop, and I volunteered.

The workshop was a trainer of trainers' workshop, and upon returning to school, much to my surprise, a six-week workshop for my fellow teachers was to be given by me. OMG, this was going to be horrible (remembering how we could be so disrespectful to presenters who came to the school). When my colleagues complimented me on how much they enjoyed my presentations, I started pondering whether this could be another role in the educational field because it was a very enjoyable experience! A position opened as a School-Based Problem-Solving facilitator, which entailed giving presentations and training to administrators and teachers. I applied for the job and was hired. In the meantime, I was married a second time but found out that he was a heavy drug user, and of course, that marriage didn't work out either.

Guess what? When they say three times is the charm, believe it! About five years later, one of my girlfriends convinced me to start dating again. We started answering and putting ads in a newspaper that posted ads for people looking for relationships. (This was before dating sites online). After meeting many frogs and princes, I finally met my King. His name is Keith Fortman. He swore I answered his ad, but that's not how I remember it! We dated for eight years before we decided to get married. During our dating season, it was discovered that he had tongue cancer. I'll never forget when the surgeon said, "You have two choices: we can cut you from ear to ear, and you will never be able to swallow again, or we can go through radiation and chemotherapy, but there are no guarantees." We were both devastated, chose radiation and chemotherapy, and relied on our faith and trust in God. After he recovered, we were married. Three years later, the unbelievable happened; he was diagnosed with prostate cancer. We are both thankful to God that he is now a two-time cancer survivor. After his recovery journey, I started my speaking career again.

One of the facilitators suggested that we return to school and get a doctorate in educational leadership. That is when and where my public speaking career blossomed. For the next ten years, I gave presentations on relationships in the workplace to administrators and educators across the United States. Public speaking was in my blood! After thirty years of working for the public school system, I retired. But what was I going to do? Definitely not sit down and do nothing. After all, I was only **65**, and as I said earlier, public speaking was in my blood!

A former colleague told me about Toastmasters International, where there would be opportunities to improve my speaking skills and speaking opportunities if I wanted to continue public speaking. But what would I do presentations on? I had no idea because I was no longer a part of the formal educational system. One day, during an evaluation of a speech, the evaluator said she noticed that most of my speeches were based on education, communication, and relationships. The more speeches I gave about communication and relationships, the more different people would ask me for advice about their communication and relationships, take my advice, and tell me it worked. Hmmm, could this be another career path? Can I be a relationship communication coach? Sometimes, you give advice, but how can you give advice when you haven't been on the same journey? So, I started looking at how I communicated, my relationships, and where I was having a problem.

My Revelation

Have you ever been in a situation where you said something and were misunderstood? How did that make you feel? What if it was someone you were remarkably close to, but how you communicated affected your relationship negatively? I was in that situation with the person I loved the most and cherished the most, My Mother. It seemed that the older I became, the way we were communicating seemed to fall apart. We argued constantly, and there were hurtful feelings on both sides. What the heck was going on? What was I missing, and how was I going to be an authentic relationship communication coach when my relationship with my mother sucked and I wasn't following my (own) advice?

This made me reflect on an experience in a meeting when I worked at Chicago Public School during a brainstorming session. We were asked to develop a program to help students improve their reading skills. When I voiced my idea, the reactions around the room indicated disinterest. A few minutes later, someone else had the same idea, which was very well received, with excitement! I thought, "Didn't I just say that?" I asked my colleague about it, and she said, "Jan, it was how you presented it. You need to communicate better, and you need to learn how to relate to people differently." I thought about this for a while; it was something my mother had told me during a misunderstanding. "Janice, it's the way you look at me, your body language, the tone of your voice." "If you want better personal and professional relationships, you better listen to what I tell you." I have a little sign on my desk that reminds me of what my mother said. It reads: "OMG, my mother was right about everything." Well, there is nothing like education, and I started reading books and taking courses on effective communication and relationships.

The first thing I wanted to do was repair my relationship with my mother. I needed to change how I communicated because I realized it takes more than words. In other words, according to what Chris Tucker said to Jackie Chan in a movie, "Do You Understand the Words That's Coming Out of My Mouth?" If you think about effective communication, that quote is more than meets the eye. I began using everything I learned about effective communication to improve my relationship with my mom. It took a while, but before she passed away, we reconciled.

One day, I talked to a group of women about how my mom and I changed our relationship from tumultuous to more loving and harmonious. They started asking me questions about how I did it. This group of women led to other women who would ask for my advice. Occasionally, a man would approach me, wanting to know how his wife or daughter could improve their relationship. I had become a relationship communication coach without knowing it! At the suggestion of some friends, I opened a coaching business and wrote a book about navigating the challenges in the adult daughter/aging mother relationship. The book is entitled "The Secrets to How NOT to Throw Mama from the Train" and has received several awards. I offer advice, solutions, comments, and humor surrounding this relationship to friends and even strangers I met along my writing journey. I started to get offers to speak at various summits, conferences, and workshops. You never know why you go through different experiences, but I believe it is training you to help and serve someone else.

The Pandemic

When the COVID-19 pandemic came around, it stopped my public speaking career, or so I thought! But what opened for me was the opportunity to speak virtually. One day, my business coach told me about an opportunity to host a podcast. This was a new form of virtual public speaking, with a format based on TV talk shows. I have always been adventurous, so I jumped at the chance at **79** years young. What I didn't know was I couldn't sit and talk. The network wanted me to interview guests! I came up with the title "Relationship Matters TV" and started having conversations with different guests about how their personal and professional relationships impacted their lives. In the beginning, the show aired/broadcasted every two weeks. It became popular, and I was convinced to do the show every week. I started broadcasting the show on an additional network. But it was taking away from my passion: mother/daughter relationship coaching. So, I decided to get on a third network focused on women and developed "The Mother/Daughter Relationship Show." On this show, I give advice, tips, and tools on how to work out the negative issues in relationships. As of this date, both shows are doing well. When the pandemic eased, opportunities to speak in person opened. I have been fortunate to speak across the United States, including Hawaii, London, Croatia, Mexico, and Jamaica.

The Adventure Continues

Earlier, I said that I was adventurous! What next?!! One day, one of my business colleagues suggested that I go on another adventure and enter a beauty contest! I laughed and said, "Girl, you must be crazy. I am a

REAL senior citizen." That's when she told me she was entering a Ms. Senior Illinois America contest and urged me to enter also. If you have ever seen a beauty pageant, what you have seen is only the surface. You have to go through some pre-qualifications before you are allowed to enter. The questionnaire is lengthy and very personal.

After I qualified to enter, there was training. We had to learn how to walk into a room, dress, apply make-up, answer the judges' questions, use body language and facial expressions, and exit the room. The judges gave you points, and if you had enough points, you were coached on how to step on a stage (with stairs) without looking at your feet and how to step on three exact points on the stage without looking at the points. I stumbled up the stairs more than once, forgot the points, and wondered how I was going to do this in a long evening gown! The next step was the actual pageant. First, there was the talent competition. I considered myself a decent singer and sang "If I Can Help Somebody, Along the Way." Then, there was the evening gown competition. Fortunately, since this was Ms. Senior Illinois America, there was no swimsuit competition (thank goodness). A man stood by as I approached the stairs to walk onto the stage. Even though I wasn't supposed to, I grabbed his hand and told him, "You ARE helping me onto this stage."

The last part of the competition is when the judges ask you one question. You must answer with as few words as possible and be straight to the point. Imagine standing there and wondering if you made any sense at all. To this day, I can't remember the question or how I answered it! Then there was the announcement of the 3rd runner-up, the 2nd runner-up, the 1st runner-up, and the winner. Much to my shock, I was crowned Ms. Senior Illinois America 2022 at **80**! After that, the Ms. Senior America 2022 competition was held in Hershey, Pennsylvania. I didn't win; however, I met many incredible women from all over the country, formed new long-term relationships, and had the opportunity to appear at several events and speak on many stages. I still receive opportunities to compete in other pageants. However, I discovered that pageant life is not for me (for reasons I will not go into).

My Journey and Adventure Continue

As I write this, I realize that the adventure is still ongoing. I was featured on a billboard in Times Square at **81**. I wrote articles for several magazines at **82**. I have two TV shows, and I am writing another book. I speak internationally, travel, facilitate Bible study, and am a lay leader in my church. I am mentoring, coaching adult daughters and their mothers, and learning everything there is to know about wines from around the world.

Someone asked me, "When will you sit down?" I answered, "For what?" As long as the good Lord says Janice, continue your journey and your adventures until I call you, that's when I will sit down. That is what I want to leave you with. Whatever you perceive, you can achieve! Whatever dream you have, pursue it! Live your life to the fullest!

One day, I was talking with my grandmother's cousin Viola, who was in her early 90's. She was sitting in a rocking chair (lotus style) and spoke. "You know Janice, I did everything I wanted to do. I didn't let anyone tell me what I couldn't do. I have lived my life just the way I wanted to. This is what I want to tell you. When you get old, I don't want you to be sitting in a rocking chair, saying to yourself, I wonder what would've happened if I could've, I wonder what would have happened if I would've. You don't want to come to the end of your life saying, I should have, would have, or could have." I have never forgotten what she said. So, I am leaving you with those exact words.

I do have one would've. "I wonder what would have happened if I had bought that horse ranch I always thought about."

Well, it's not too late!

About The Author

Dr. Janice Hooker-Fortman

Dr. Janice Hooker-Fortman is a renowned relationship coach and author who is highly celebrated for her expertise in effective communication dynamics. With over 20 years of experience, Dr. Jan has become a leading voice in transforming interpersonal relationships. Her unique approach combines practical communication strategies with deep psychological insights, empowering individuals to foster healthier, more fulfilling personal and professional connections.

Her charismatic presence extends to television, where she hosts the popular show "Relationship Matters TV." She has impactful conversations with her guests, focusing on how their relationships have impacted their personal and professional lives. The show is educational, inspirational, and entertaining.

Internationally recognized, Dr. Jan is a sought-after speaker known for her engaging and insightful presentations, in which she shares her expertise on relationship dynamics and communication strategies. Dr. Fortman is about solving problems and nurturing understanding, empathy, and connection to improve relationships.

At **80**, she was crowned Ms. Senior Illinois America 2022. When not speaking, she enjoys traveling with her husband Keith, a two-time cancer survivor, and supporting her son Kevin in his videography and photography business.

Contact Dr. Jan at:
Email: DrJan@DrJanice-Fortman.com

7

The Sixty-Seven Percent

Dr. Renita Gibbs

Imagine being a child of a single-parent home, growing into an adult, and being overwhelmed with questions of your origin. This is my story. I was part of the 67%. The 67% is the number associated with African American children that are raised in single-parent homes. I felt like that number plagued me throughout my life. Growing up in a home with just my sister and mother, I felt incomplete.

My mother did an exceptional job raising both my sister and me. However, I could not stop wondering about my father. I yearned to know him. I had a strong desire to understand who he was. Which, for me, would bring some clarity to who I was. Being part of the 67% is so common that many children grow into acceptance of the number and normalize the condition. It is easy to do. When you have so many others around you living in the same circumstances, I, however, could not accept this. So, as an adult, I began a search. A search for answers, a search for my daddy!

I had no idea how this search would turn out or what I would learn along this journey. I did not know that my mother or sister would not support my decision. I had no idea that things I grew up believing would be revealed to be untrue. Finally, I did not know the pain and disappointment I would experience and how this would shape my life into a joy I could cherish and share with many. Those in the 67% and those not a part of that group more than likely would forge bonds, friendships, and marriages with those who were and may need some understanding.

I had not seen or heard from my father since I was a little girl. The last time I saw him, we were in a courthouse. My mother had him summoned there to determine the paternity of my sister and me. I remember the judge telling him that he was the man responsible for fathering my sister and me. She ordered him to provide support. Once the court proceedings were over, we all returned to the home I shared with my sister and mother. My daddy took my sister and me to McDonald's, where he talked to us for some time. We returned home, and he talked to us on the porch for a little longer. I cannot recall much of the conversation. I remember that before he left, he had promised my sister and me he would stay in touch with us. Then he left, and we never saw him again.

I moved through life guided by my mother's hand. I made it through high school. I went on to college, eventually met my future husband, got married, and started my own family. I had not settled into life. A part of me was still that little girl on that porch many years ago, left with the promise of seeing my father again. Growing up, we did not discuss my father. The little things I did know I held onto. My mother told us he was in the military, which was the reason my sister and I went to the military base for health care. I knew she received a monthly check for my sister and me because she always commented that the money was insufficient. Not for two girls. I also knew she said I was built with a high butt like my father. I did not know what that meant, but I would look at myself in the mirror, studying myself, trying to associate other features with the man who left us on the porch that day.

As an adult, knowing what I know now, I think my mother's comment about me being built like my father was more in reference to my steely attitude. I certainly displayed this trait in the search for my father. My mother and sister would ridicule my efforts and try to discourage me from seeking out a man who left me standing on a porch waiting for him to return. They could not detour me from my search. I was determined to find this man. To find that piece of myself that had been missing all these years.

There are some things that, in hindsight, I can admit, like the fact that I never considered how my persistence in finding my daddy made my mother feel. I'm sure at some point, she questioned herself regarding her hand in raising us. I probably made her think (as if) she had not done an excellent job, which is not the case. She also may have felt a slight disappointment as a woman. In the sense that this is a man, she had to go to court to determine paternity of her children. Why would her daughter seek out a man she had to force to take care of his responsibility?

Finding my daddy was something that consumed me. I started finding myself thinking about it throughout my daily life. I watch my children interact with my husband, see other families out and about, and watch family-based TV shows. Almost anything would trigger me. Once I started my search, I was not prepared for the disappointment I would encounter. The first disappointment came from my mother, who was totally against me seeking this man out. She would say, 'What are you expecting to find?" 'You're looking for someone who should be looking for you!' 'Do you think that man is thinking about you?' 'All you're going to find is a man who wants nothing to do with you.' These words hurt, but I did not let those words break my spirit.

I don't believe my mother ever came to an understanding as to why finding my father meant so much to me. Still, I think my relentless attitude toward finding him wore her down, and she eventually gave me the information I needed to start seeking my daddy out actively. I took the information and hit the ground running with nothing but the support of my husband, who had been understanding and sympathetic the entire time.

I first reached out to the military base where my sister and I used to go for our checkups. The military had records of me and my sister, and they did let me know that my father was still living. I was relieved to find this out because I did not know if he was still living. They also dealt me my next disappointment. I learned that my father had a wife and two other children. I cannot lie. Learning this made me think about all the negative things my mother had said about my search.

I took some time to process this new information. I was hurt and confused. I talked to my husband about it for weeks before he convinced me it changed nothing. This was still my daddy, and I still needed to find him in order to cure the sickness that not having him around had caused me. I overcame my disappointment and welcomed the fact that I had two other sisters I did not know about.

I contacted the military base again and attempted to get an address or number for my father. They refused to give me any information over the phone. They said I would have to show up in person to present proper identification, and then they (maybe) could assist me. I spoke with my husband and told him of my plan to go to the military base to follow up. He encouraged me to go right away. I am unsure if his encouragement came from wanting me to find my daddy or end my search. I know my actions had to have come off as obsessive. I certainly was showing some neglect toward my own family. However, I did not notice it at the time.

I flew to North Carolina, the last place my father was stationed. I was nervous the entire time. I rented a car and headed to the military base. I tried to control my nerves as I spoke with the woman in the records department. I did not feel at ease until she handed me a piece of paper with an address and phone number. I left the office feeling a strong sense of excitement, only for the nervousness to resurface when I dialed the number on the paper. The number was a working number, but no one answered the phone. I tried calling again, but still no answer. The woman in the records department told me that my father was retired, so I wondered where he could be. Was he away on vacation?

I decided to drive to the address on the paper. I came too far to get on a plane and return home with a piece of paper. The address was about forty minutes away from the military base. I arrived and sat in my car in front of his house for a long time. I looked up and down the street. I don't know what I was looking for, but I just sat there. A million thoughts ran through my mind. What if his wife answered the door? What would I say? What was I going to say if he answered the door? I convinced myself to get out of the car and walk up to the house. My nerves were jumping all over the place.

I pressed the doorbell and waited. Nothing, no one came to the door. I pressed the bell again, and I heard movement inside this time. Finally, the door opened, and a frail older man with a humpback stared at me. I studied his face and saw my sister's eyes glaring back at me. I knew I had found my daddy. He asked if he could help me. I stood there in a trance-like state until he asked again. I asked if he knew who I was, and he replied, "No." I then spoke my full name. At that point, he looked at me, and I could see tears forming in his eyes. He fell into my arms and hugged me.

I found my daddy! This was a bittersweet moment that I had been waiting for. The reason is that just three months later, my father fell ill and ended up in ICU. At this time, I would meet his wife, whom he had separated from. I would also meet my half-sister. He had already told me that my other half-sister had become ill and passed away shortly before I reunited with him. He said that he felt like God had blessed him by bringing me and my sister back into his life after losing a child.

His wife and other daughter were unhappy about me being back in my father's life. I realized this firsthand when I came to the hospital to see him. I was told I would no longer be admitted into the ICU. His wife was the executor of his estate and got a court order to prevent anyone from seeing him without their permission. My father had another woman with whom he was with at the time. She had been his sole caregiver up until the point he was placed in ICU. She was not allowed to see him either. His wife and daughter had no sympathy or care that we loved this man and wanted to be by his side. They did not care about the lengths I had to endure to find my daddy. They came off as bitter and evil. Three months after being admitted into the ICU and six months after reuniting with him, my daddy died. I was broken, crushed! I felt like that little girl on the porch again. I felt like God had cheated me.

The short time with my father was bittersweet. I was happy I was able to reconnect with him and find a piece of myself that I felt had been missing, but I felt I needed more time with him. I realized that my search for my father had been my biggest hurdle in life. I learned through this journey that I could overcome any challenge in life. This experience became my testimony. I began to speak about it to people close to me, in the church, and in other areas of my life.

I realized this connection with my father opened my eyes to the many other fatherless children like me. I was interested in connecting with others who may be suffering from the same feelings I had been dealing with before reconnecting with my father. I felt like my story could help and encourage others to cope with an undercover identity crisis that is rarely talked about out loud. I wanted to extend my testimony beyond the church, my circle of friends and family, beyond my own community.

I figured the way to do this was to tell my story through a book. I could reach many more people that way. I wasted no time writing down notes and preparing the structure for what would become *Finding Daddy*. I worked on this novel every free moment I had. Once it was complete, I contacted a friend with some publishing experience. This person helped me get my book published, and just like that, I formed another connection with my father. This book would ensure that he was forever a part of me.

The book was just the first part of a new journey. As I expressed, I wanted to connect with others who had also been raised in fatherless homes and children who were currently living through this reality. I began speaking in libraries and other literary events. I was surprised at how many people wanted to connect with me and how many people my story resonated with. Before long, I received invites from different groups and organizations who wanted me to appear at their events and tell my story.

I traveled all over the United States, appearing on stages in front of thousands. I would tell my story repeatedly, and it never got old. When I exited these stages, I was approached by many people who wanted to speak with me. I found myself talking to people I had met through emails and personal phone calls. I decided to form a mentorship program, which allowed me to transition into a family child advocate coach. I eventually formed my company, "Fresh Wisdom," which aimed to lift the spirits of people (old and young) who were struggling with being fatherless children. There were so many people out there who could relate to my story and those who had their own stories that needed to be told and heard.

My objective was to expose some of the key issues that lie beneath the surface of childhood trauma. These are the issues that are often never spoken about or overlooked. When people examine dysfunction that exists in youth, that sometimes transitions into adulthood. I wanted to be a living example for people to view and understand that they could overcome and release the pinned-up emotions they tried so hard to disguise. `

I wanted to use the platform I built as a talking point to encourage others to open up and speak about the lifelong effects of fatherlessness. Many people do not even realize this is an issue because it has been normalized throughout society. The 67% gets inflated by the ignorance of not recognizing this is a problem. I want to shed light on this issue and create a safety net. I want to give insight into the importance of vetting men and women correctly to deflate the overwhelming number in terms of family and proper structure.

I want to expel the myth that being a single parent is okay, and it is not. Being a single parent is often not a choice, but we must understand the effects that being a single parent can have on a child. Without doing so, we ignore the signs of depression, psychological defects, character and attachment issues, abandonment issues, filling voids by over-sexualization, and other dysfunctional behaviors. Here, I am focused more on the child, not the adult who has possibly already suffered this trauma into adulthood. At some point, we must focus on prevention to break the cycle.

I have been blessed to meet some very good people along this journey. One person in particular who was interested in my message and what I was doing was the world-renowned motivational speaker Les Brown. Communicating with him and seeing his interest in my work motivated me even more and made me want to broaden my horizons. I continued to mentor people and pour into my program, "Fresh Wisdom," but I started exploring the existence of this issue beyond the United States.

I began researching this issue on a global scale, and I was surprised to realize that this was not just an issue that existed in our nation but an international one. There were children in India, China, Canada, and many other places who were a part of the 67%. The numbers may vary from place to place, but the effects seemed the same. I started making motivational reels to speak on the issues, and it was not long before my voice became international. I was receiving emails and messages from people all over the world.

I was beyond excited when I was invited to visit and speak at a school in Cape Town, South Africa. I was not sure what to expect, but what I realized was this trauma was just as impactful in this country as it was in our own. The one thing that surprised me the most was that it was not just the students I had the pleasure of meeting and speaking to but also the teachers in the school who had grown into adulthood, living and suffering from this same trauma. These women praised me for my courage and openness, but more than that, they were hoping and expecting me to provide a solution. This was eye-opening and made me realize that my work is far from being done. I have so much more to do and so many more people to reach. I still am, and will always be, part of the 67%, but I am going to keep it a hundred on the issue and strive to be a cure for the trauma that exists because of it.

About The Author

Dr. Renita Gibbs

Dr. Renita Gibbs is a native of Augusta, Georgia, and is currently residing in Atlanta, Georgia. Dr. Gibbs is a successful entrepreneur, a "Fatherless Daughter" Advocate, and a Life Coach. Her goal is to empower and encourage women who have not had fathers in their lives. Dr. Gibbs seeks opportunities to extend to young ladies the tools of liberation and freedom from the feeling of bondage, rejection, and co-dependency. Dr. Gibbs's focus is to have women personally dismantle the mental bondage and take up the torch of knowledge, wisdom, strength, and courage to rise above the obstacles and pull from deep within themselves to believe and cause to manifest the dreams that lie within.

Dr. Gibbs is an Inspirational Speaker and has been the keynote speaker throughout the United States and Africa. She facilitates weekly training and coaching seminars, preparing participants for successful outreach and mentorship with youth in local communities.

Dr. Gibbs has become a strong voice in many communities through her passion, work, and relentless commitment. She is looking for individuals who desire support and are willing to take the challenge of journeying on a healthier life path and carving out better opportunities for future generations.

Dr. Gibbs stands on integrity and places God first in everything she does. She is available for speaking engagements, seminars, and workshops. She is ready to facilitate any function geared toward Fatherless Daughters, family, and relationships. Dr. Gibbs' motto is "Integrity Counts."

Testimonial for Dr. Gibbs

I have had the pleasure of knowing and working with Renita Gibbs for the past 13 years. I have witnessed her take her first title, Finding Daddy, to heights few new authors reach. She committed herself to spreading a message through her literary works, allowing her to expand and form new platforms to get her message out to the masses. ***Author Aaron Bebo.***

8

It's God's Plan

Catherine Phillips-Hogan

I was born in a small rural area called Baxter County, Arkansas, on September 2, 1951. Baxter County is around 108 miles from Little Rock, the Capital City. Here's a bit of history for you. The Baxter Vidette, an African American Newspaper, began publishing in my hometown (Baxter, Arkansas) in 1902, 49 years before I was born. The newspaper was published semi-monthly by J.G. Robinson and W.H. Grey. The year I was born (1951), a shortage of state funds caused the Cotter school system to close in April.

My parents' names were James R. and Jessie M. Phillips. So, there you have it, Jessie James. I was raised on a farm in a home with only four rooms (called a shotgun house)—early construction of shotgun houses did not include indoor bathrooms. A front porch and a back porch were attached to the home, and one room was extending on the right side of the house. The roof was made from tin, which made me very sleepy from hearing the rain fall on the flat rooftop. You could stand in the front door of our home and see straight through to the kitchen. It was like looking down the barrel of a shotgun, straight sight from front to back. Shotgun houses were popular in the Southern United States after the Civil War, around 1861 through the 1920s.

The first room was the living room and the bedroom for my parents. The second room was the dining room, which later became the bedroom for my brothers. The third room was the kitchen, and the right-sided attached room was also there. The fourth room was my room, alone after I got older. I was the third of four siblings. Notice I did not mention having a bathroom in our shotgun house.

My mother and father were poor farmers trying to make a living for the family using any honest means possible. Poor farmers in Baxter County, Arkansas, had small production compared to large farms. My mother and father would do business with whatever and whoever came around to purchase their crops because they had little alternative. We all lived and worked on Uncle Robert's farm.

Living on Uncle Robert's farm as children was fun. We had a lot of space to run and play. Yes, believe it or not, we still found time to play after we finished our chores. Uncle Robert was old-fashioned and did not believe in updated amenities. We used kerosene lamps because Uncle Robert would not agree to sign for the electric company to dig and put the electric poles on his property. We did not have electricity until I was in eleventh grade. We thought there was a lot of light in our home as we were doing our homework, but when we got the electric lights, it seemed like daylight (in the house) at night. I am surprised we did not need eyeglasses as children or adults! Thank God!

We had an outdoor toilet, referred to as an "outhouse." We had to take a bath in what was called a number two tin tub. We didn't have running water in our home. We had a pump drilled down to a running water stream in the ground. The pump was outside, about five hundred feet from our home. We carried water into the house with a water bucket, which resembled today's foot tub but was smaller. Relatives from various parts of the country, mainly Chicago, would visit us and tell us our water was salty. We could not taste the salt in the water because it was what we were used to drinking. After I graduated from high school and came back home to visit, true enough, the water did taste salty.

Because we had no electricity, we finally got an icebox. My parents had to catch a ride to town from a neighbor with a vehicle and buy hot ice. Once we purchased the hot ice, someone from the ice store would bring it to our home. We could not touch the hot ice with bare hands. The delivery man used (something like) big hooks to take the ice from the truck and put it in the ice box. We were all happy with that ice box. We had cold water, milk, Kool-Aid, etc.

Next, we got a butane gas tank, which enabled us to go from a wood stove to a butane one. Boy! What a difference. We later got running water in the kitchen and a sink. We could wash dishes in the sink rather than in a dish pan.

I started elementary school at six years old. I had to walk about a mile to the main road to board the school bus. After getting home from school, we had to get out of our school clothes, put on our work clothes, eat, and head for the field or garden. So, you see, our rural life was hard. It consisted of gardening, farming, and raising animals. We worked Monday through Saturday, helping our parents keep food on the table and earn an income from time to time. On Sundays, we had to attend church. After church, we got to play and have fun with the other children in the community.

We had to walk about a mile and a half to church. We would have fun playing as we went to church, but we knew not to be late! My father developed heart disease. He would get shortness of breath. Therefore, he could not walk to church often. Sometimes, he would try, but we had to make many stops along the way. We were happy he was with us.

My mother could attend church more often than Daddy, mainly on the fourth Sunday. On the fourth Sunday, we would be in church all day. This was also fun! All the sisters at the church would fix food and bring it to the church in boxes. That food was delicious! All the food from my mother's box would disappear first. My Mama was known to be the best cook in town!

After Sunday School, the children would play until it was time to eat before the next service started. There weren't enough Pastors, so our Pastor could only come out to church on the fourth Sunday. He would go to different churches on the other Sundays of the month. This was called a Circuit Preacher. So, Mama and Daddy would try to be at church on the fourth Sunday. The rest of the Sundays, we would have Sunday school. My Mama would come to Sunday school sometimes. She basically would stay at home with Daddy. Mama would have dinner ready for us when we got home. We were not allowed to eat at other neighbors' houses because they had several children and should not have to feed us, too. The neighbors would ask us to stay for dinner so we could play with their children, but we dared not to say yes because we would be in big trouble when we got home. Sometimes, if Mama were with us, she would visit with her friends, who had children, and we would all eat together. We would reciprocate this, and different neighbors would do the same.

We had a cast iron stove for cooking our meals and two tin heaters, which heated the house in the winter. Later, my parents got a cast iron heater for the living room/their bedroom, but there was still a tin heater in my room. The cast iron heater and stove held heat longer and got hotter.

Our daddy showed us how to cut down trees for wood. There was a way to do it to keep the saw from binding and the tree from falling the wrong way. The saw that we used had two handles; one person was on each end of the saw. After the tree was cut down, the limbs had to be cut off from the tree. The tree would then be sawed up into small blocks, and the blocks would be split into firewood. Sometimes, we would borrow our cousin Willie's wagon and mule team to haul the wood to the house. When we could not use the wagon, we had to make many trips into the woods to carry the wood home. Hard work!

I started chopping and picking cotton at eight years old. People who could afford to pay us for day work would use our services and pay us a dollar daily. They would pay adults a little more than children. During my childhood, there was no such thing as child labor laws, and we worked and worked and worked. Even though we were free, I felt like a slave doing backbreaking work for free or little of nothing in return.

My life was hard on the farm, but I was determined that one day, I would be somebody who did not have to struggle to live. My mother and father always managed to feed, clothe, and show us they loved us. They wanted us to do better than they did in life. We would talk and laugh around the table as we shared our food. That was a must! We had to sit around the table for breakfast, lunch, and dinner. This was family time, where we had serious talks and fun talks. We loved our parents and appreciated them.

When we got electricity, I was in eleventh grade, and boy, was I one happy camper! Before we got electricity, I had to do homework with kerosene lamps. The kerosene had a distinctive oily, pungent smell that I will never forget.

One of the most challenging things that happened when I was growing up was when my father became ill. The doctor informed him that he could never work again. This was devastating to the family. My father did not know what to do. This farming was how he provided for the family. Daddy was an enormously proud man. He did not want to get on welfare but realized my mother could not provide for the family by herself. He agreed to apply for welfare, and we qualified to get it. It made life somewhat easier. I think this was part of God's Plan.

I went to Chicot County High School and graduated in 1969. I moved to Forsyth, Georgia. I stayed with my sister and her family for three years. I worked at a luggage company and a sheet factory. I realized I had more to offer than working long hours in a factory for the rest of my life. I have always wanted to be a nurse, and this has not helped me reach that goal. After speaking with one of my aunts, she told me she could get me into nursing school if I came and lived with her in Chicago. She worked at one of the well-known hospitals in Chicago. I believed her.

I moved to Chicago, Illinois, in 1972. I quickly got a job at a file and index company. While working full-time there, I went to Automation Academy and got a certificate in Key punching. I got a part-time night job at Evan Fur Store, Key punching. I still knew this was not my calling.

Well, my aunt didn't do what she said she would do. I learned that my aunt always wanted me to be her daughter. She asked my mother if she would give me to her, because she had been unsuccessful at having children for my uncle. Of course, my Mama said no, but she remained one of my favorite aunts.

There was a pause in my education because, by this time, I had met and married a Chicago Transit Bus Operator. We had a little girl in 1975. We had a baby girl named Cherie. When Cherie was ten months old, I started furthering my education at Loop Jr. College, now known as Harold Washington College. I received an associate degree, but I still did not have what I needed. I believed this was also part of God's plan for my life.

I had no friends and was unfamiliar with the South Side of Chicago. Remember, I was a country girl living in the big city. I was determined to succeed and had to make my way the best I could. I found out that I could apply to Loyola University Nursing School. I did, and I was accepted into their Nursing Program. It did not work out like I thought it would. I was faced with a lot of prejudice and racism from some of the teachers and the Director of Nursing, who was a Catholic Nun. I expected her to be different because of her religious values, but I was as wrong as two left shoes. In my reading of the Bible, one of my favorite scriptures was Romans 8:28; "We know that all things work together for the good of those who love God who are called according to his purpose." God can still work things out for my good, even with the challenges I faced.

I kept finding my way until I was about to enter my junior year. My personal life began to take a toll, and I started to have marital issues. I had to leave the nursing program because of the pain and suffering that caused me a bit of trauma. I was devastated. I did not know what to do. An older friend talked with me and told me that she thought I would be a great social worker and still have the same direct contact with the patients in the hospital. She spoke of the qualities that she felt I had and encouraged me to try it. She was familiar with the school system and informed me how to change my major.

I made an appointment to see the Dean of Students the next day. The Dean wanted to know what was going on with me. I informed him, and he assisted me with precisely what I should do and how to do it. My Spirit was lifted, and I was happy once again! I thanked the Dean and my friend. I discovered that this is where God always wanted me to be. All my life appeared to fall into place and fit like a puzzle! Here is the critical factor: I went from surviving the issues in my marriage to thriving because God, my Higher Power, kept His hands on me. According to God's plan, every challenge had a lesson for me to learn. I became stronger and more determined to stay focused on the path set for me.

I was working at a Doctor's Hospital as a Social Worker Assistant. My boss decided to promote me. I was given the title of Social Worker. My boss stated that I was doing an excellent job and had the innate qualities to be a social worker. But I needed schooling to know why I was doing what I was doing. I continued to attend Loyola University School of Social Work. I graduated from Loyola with a master's degree in social work on May 11, 1996, and a bachelor's degree from DePaul University on June 14, 1987. My major was Sociology, my minor was in Health and Human Services, and I earned my Associate of Arts Degree from Loop Jr. College on May 17, 1980.

Can you believe that the daughter of poor farmers from Baxter County, Arkansas, who lived in a shotgun house, grew up working and living on her Uncle Robert's farm, walking a mile to school, and now is a College Graduate from Chicago's Loyola University with a master's degree in social work? Yes, that's me, Catherine Phillips-Hogan, the author/writer of this chapter. Let's get back to My Life, My Story.

I continued to work at Doctors Hospital. My boss quit her current position for more money and responsibilities and recommended me for her old position. I accepted the position and became the Director of Social Services. My master's degree qualified me to be employed in this higher-paying, higher-responsibility position.

While working at Doctors' Hospital, the patients started asking me to come into their homes to help them with things they couldn't or had difficulty doing. I could not do it myself, but I explained that I could help them get the services they needed in their homes. Some would agree, and some would not agree because they wanted me and me alone to be the ones who provided the in-home service. I could see where God was leading me.

There would come a time when some of the patients could no longer live in their homes alone. They needed 24-hour care to live in their homes. They could not afford to pay a healthcare provider to stay with them because in-home healthcare services were expensive. They had no other choice but to be placed in a nursing facility. They would look at me and say, with tears in their eyes, Mrs. Hogan, If I go to a Nursing Home, I will "die." This would break my heart whenever I heard this statement from a patient. God gave me a compassionate and caring heart. I felt so helpless. I thought taking them home with me would be alright, but I knew that was impossible.

I knew, and the patient knew that there was no other choice but for them to be placed in a nursing home. They could not take care of themselves and could not live alone. If the patient had someone outside of the hospital to assist them with placement, I would give the patients their family, friends, or loved ones a listing of nursing homes and ask them to pick three nursing homes to visit. They could visit any nursing home until they found a facility they liked for the patient to be placed in. I went above and beyond the call of duty to assist with helping patients find the best nursing home that fit their needs.

I would have the Director of Admission come over to speak with the patient and tell them about their facility and what they had to offer them. The marketing person would bring pictures of the facility and inform the patients what they had to offer. This helped the patients feel somewhat better, but they were going because they had to.

I went to visit nursing homes to see what they were like. If the patient had no one to assist them, I would tell them about the nursing home I visited, give them information and pamphlets, and have the Director of the Nursing Home come out to talk with them. The patients were encouraged to ask questions. The patients would choose the nursing home they felt was best for them.

The hospital went through some changes and was about to close. I knew my time working at this hospital was soon coming to an end. I applied for a Social Worker position in the Cook County Hospital System. I worked at Provident Hospital of Cook County at 500 East 51 Street on Chicago's Southside for sixteen years. I later transferred to John H. Stroger Hospital of Cook County (The Old County Hospital) at 1969 West Ogden Ave on Chicago's Westside. I worked there for ten years. At these two hospitals, patients started having the same talk with me as they did at Doctor's Hospital. They were crying out to me for help. I knew I had to do something about it.

I spoke with a good friend of mine, Lolita Terry, who encouraged me to start a program that would help patients stay out of the nursing home and stay in their homes. Lolita stated that she would help me, so we got started. I went to Lolita's house one night after I got off work. We started burning the midnight oil to make things right for our patients. We formed our legal entity and picked a name for the business. We listed our overall objectives, mission statement, and how we would get funds to start the business.

Life for Seniors Inc. was born! We were so happy that all the paperwork was completed. We were approved as a not-for-profit and received our 501(C)3 from the State of Illinois on May 5, 2000. Now, it was time for the real work to begin. Life for Seniors Inc. applied for a state grant and qualified for it. Emil Jones Jr., President of the Illinois Senate, believed in our vision and allotted us two hundred and fifty thousand dollars. Most of the grant money was put into the services provided to the patients.

My friend and co-partner of the business received a small salary. Sometimes, I would accept a small stipend or allowance because I worked full-time, and my co-partner did not work. She donated her services full-time to the office to keep it running smoothly. We also moved into a small office and got the supplies and equipment needed to run the office. We had several volunteers. We were thankful for them. They were accommodating. My friend Lolita ran the business side of the office. She had a bachelor's degree in business, and I arranged and set up the services because I was a licensed social worker. We did great! We had enough patients. The patients and their families loved the workers that we hired. We hired our workers as contractors to stretch the funds. We knew we didn't have enough funds to pay insurance for the workers.

The State sent someone to inspect the office and ensure the grant money was being spent on its stated purpose. The man from the State finished so quickly that my partner and I were looking at each other. He left for a while and came back to the office. He told us that he was finished. He said, "Never have I seen books for a not-for-profit, so in tack, you have every penny accounted for and the proof to go along with it." We were surprised to hear him say that most not-for-profit companies don't have records, and the money is spent on stuff that should not have been.

Our funds were getting low, but they were well spent. We applied for another grant from the State. At first, we were denied more grant money. Then, after consideration and speaking with Emil Jones Jr., we were granted an additional seventy-five thousand dollars. Unfortunately, we did not receive this money because a new governor was elected. Every time we called about the funds, we were told it was on the Governor's desk. Well, we eventually gave up trying to get the money. I guess it stayed on the Governor's desk because it never reached our desk.

Well, here comes the other "Potholes in the Road." After 9-11, 2001, we couldn't get any more money. We were only able to offer referral services. The person we rented the office allowed us to stay two extra months. He said we were good customers and always paid our rent on time. He also said that he believed in what we were doing. We kept all our paperwork up to date and continued trying to survive. We eventually had to close.

Former employees and customers continued to call to see if we were open again because they enjoyed working for us, and the customers loved the services they received. Even though we were closed, I couldn't give up. I knew the services were severely needed, but we could not get the funds to reopen our non-profit. I kept the paperwork and everything the business required to operate up to date. I knew when the right time came, God would open the doors. I would ask God, "What are you teaching me?" "Why isn't this working?" Whenever I wanted to give up, something would happen to tell me that the services were still needed.

Other "Potholes in the Road" happened. In 2010, I had an aneurysm and recovered quickly from that traumatic experience. Everyone at the hospital where I was employed could not believe I was still alive, including the doctors and nurses.

In 2018, my husband and I were returning home, and the camper rolled over twice. We had minor injuries. I had a broken arm, and my husband was thrown out of the camper. No other vehicle was involved. Look at God! As the camper was about to roll over, I cried, "God to save us!" As the camper continued to roll over, I said, "God, I ask you to save us." I heard a still voice saying to me, "I did." I was driving the camper. The camper rolled over on the driver's side. I couldn't get out the door. The fire department had to cut me out of the camper with the "Jaws of Life."

We were transported to the Trauma Center in Memphis, Tennessee. The Nurse notified our daughter and son. They both flew down to Memphis immediately. My husband was in the ICU for one week due to surgery for a blood clot. I was treated for a broken arm, which was very painful, and was released from the Emergency Room. After my broken arm had been set, I fell asleep from all the trauma that I had gone through that day.

When I woke up, I saw two smiling faces at the foot of my bed. They were my cousins. I was so happy to see them! I had forgotten that I had relatives in Memphis, Tennessee. I went home with them. They picked our children up from the airport. They didn't live far from the hospital or the airport. Look at God! We could all stay in my cousin's home, which had plenty of room, until we were ready to return to Chicago. We had to rent a vehicle because our camper was totaled. I started to faint when we looked at the camper after they towed it. I saw the mercy and grace of my God. Again, this was all part of God's plan for my life.

I didn't tell you. My husband had already been diagnosed with cancer. One of the worst kinds is Renal Cell Carcinoma. He had to have his left kidney removed. He almost died from the surgery, but God! My husband lived 20 years with cancer. He was always upbeat and would not let anyone talk negatively to him, not even the doctors. Everyone on his healthcare team came to respect him and was happy to see him when he went into the office and clinics for treatment. His health started to deteriorate. He could hardly walk, but he kept moving. It finally got where I had become his primary caregiver at 69 years old. Can you imagine how I had to care for him like a baby? He later had to be placed in Hospice. We still laughed and talked to each other. We had all the medical equipment needed to make life somewhat more manageable as I continued to care for him.

Our daughter, granddaughter, and his son would come by when they could. They had to work, and our granddaughter was in school. My husband finally could not take it anymore. He passed away not from cancer but from a disease called Dysphagia. He could no longer eat or swallow. He got so small in a month. So, it got (really) personal for me when my husband got sick, and I had to take care of him. My husband was my senior by a few years. So, you can imagine how difficult this road was for me. But God! I made it!

This journey made it more convincing to me. It made me more determined to stay on my mission to help the frail and sick elderly remain in their home to live as independently as possible, viable within their communities, and at the end of their life's journey, they can die with dignity and respect.

MY MESSAGE TO YOU

Here is the critical factor: I went from surviving the issues in my life to thriving because God, my Higher Power, kept His hands on me. If I can turn my adversities into greatness, despite my challenges, and continue to find a way to help and serve others, YOU CAN, TOO!

–Catherine Phillips–Hogan

About The Author

Catherine Phillips–Hogan

Catherine Phillips-Hogan is the President/CEO of Life for Seniors Inc. She was born in Dermott, Arkansas, and is the third of four children. She attended DePaul University in Chicago, Illinois, for her bachelor's degree and graduated with a major in sociology and a minor in health and human services. She then received a master's degree from Loyola University, Chicago, Illinois, and graduated with a major in Social Work. After over 25 years of social work experience, she successfully transitioned into her current Life for Seniors Inc. role. She is currently the Founder's President/CEO of Life for Seniors Inc.

9

Failure Isn't Final But Royalty Is Forever

Sherri Britton

After discovering that failure isn't final and experiencing so many life lessons, I realized that what we call failure isn't a failure unless you quit. Failure is the step that takes us into our GREATNESS AND VICTORY, from our visions, dreams, and goals to life's achievements and success. Failure is all a part of everyone's life. We must learn to live life and not allow life to live us.

Everyone has a story. Its design is to give God All the Glory. As we trust and believe, we will come out on top, and there's always victory. If you don't stop, don't quit, you will win. Winners never quit, and quitters never win! Look at all the stories of people's lives that went from tragedy to triumph. They were abandoned or rejected by their parents or family. Some experienced more severe issues than others.

Take Abraham Lincoln, for instance. He was born in adverse poverty, lived in a log cabin, and was extremely poor. His stepmother told him to read as many books as he could. Lincoln became a self-taught lawyer. He ran for Senate multiple times but failed. His sweetheart died. Lincoln had a nervous breakdown and knew if he did not give up, the key to success would be hard work and determination. Lincoln became the 16th President of THE UNITED STATES OF AMERICA after many atrocities, one being rejected by his parents.

Steve Jobs was raised by his adoptive parents, Paul and Clara Jobs. At age 21, Apple Computer Inc. was founded on April 1, 1976, by college dropouts. Steve Jobs and Steve Wozniak brought to the new company a vision of changing how people viewed computers. However, in 1985, Jobs was fired, and he was so innovative that he started his own company. Steve Jobs's estimated net worth was over 10 billion dollars, and most of his wealth went to his wife, Laurene Powell Jobs, and his first daughter, Lisa Brennan-Jobs.

Failure is a part of life's process, pain, problems, and promises along our journey to achieve our goals, dreams, and visions. No one is exempt from problems, pain, and failure. It's not what happens to you in life. It's how you respond to it that matters most.

Death of a loved one, spouse, father, mother, child, divorce, loss of job, and loss of financial security are inevitable in the lives of many. It happens to the best of us. Validated failure will never happen if we Don't Stop, Don't Quit, and Don't Look Back. We must keep treading through the good, the bad, and the ugly. The question is, ONLY when we quit can we verify failure to be an absolute failure?

About 35 years ago, Sherri Britton learned that pain births fourth purpose. Coming out of a broken home of abuse and divorce, I was constantly teased that I was dumb, stupid, crazy, and off. However, I chose to be happy, no matter what people said about me. My dad abused my mother, and he would beat her. He gave her a black eye, called her out of her name, and told her how worthless she was. He stole her money. He told her that she had ugly blemishes on her face and that she was not as good-looking as he was. He didn't know how to be a father because his father wasn't a good example of a father to him. He grew up with my grandfather constantly beating my grandmother. One weekend, when my father had me and my two siblings over, I experienced my grandfather beating my grandmother, and she was crying and screaming, stop, don't!

My grandmother was beautiful and extremely pleasant, although she had a mental illness. So, when she didn't do what my grandfather wanted, he would beat her. My siblings and I were terrified while crying for our mother. Picture this: three children in the bedroom left alone to sleep while my father ran the streets to be with other women. My grandfather did the same with my grandmother during his cycle of abuse.

I struggled in school in almost every subject because of the trauma from the dysfunctional abuse. I felt like I had no value or self-worth. I was an overly sensitive child. After seeing my father mistreat my mother and laughing about it, I began to worry as a child. I never wanted to be treated like that. When my father started trying to beat us, my mother would always stand in the way and take our beatings. I struggled through school and graduated.

Finally, I got married, thinking all the abuse would end and I would live life happily ever after. WRONG!!! I experienced generational abuse, in many ways like my mother had, being called the B word. I would get dressed up, expecting to go out, only to find out my husband wanted to go out with his friends instead of me. I didn't drink or smoke, so I guess I was called boring or square. The children and I were left alone at home again. It was not a wholesome family, just like it was with my dad and mom.

There's a father, there's a mother, and there are children. We were not connected as a whole family. We were merely existing. We were not living as a family enjoying life, going to the park, zoo, or library to enhance our family relationship of love and bonding. Instead, I heard a statement like, I want my wife and (my) girlfriend. I was devastated, insulted, jealous, angry, and shocked that he would have the nerve to think that I was so desperate to have him under those conditions. I would lower my standards and share my husband with another woman...No, definitely not. I told him he needed to make a choice.

Enough is enough. Yes, I said it because I was angry. But I did not mean it. I thought I was still in love with him, but I found out later that I wasn't in love at all! I was infatuated for eleven years, thinking I was in love. True love goes beyond mere attraction or infatuation. Love is an intense feeling of deep affection. It's the act of caring and giving to someone else, prioritizing someone's best interests and well-being in your life. To truly love is a very selfless act.

I received those acts of kindness when we first began our relationship. His sword faded away. I prayed that he would come to his senses and that we could be that happy-ever-after couple for a lifetime. I didn't know what love was, so I was holding on to an empty dream and a colorless rainbow. That's how many people get stuck in their lives, thinking they have the real thing when it's only a façade. I did not know how to let him go. I was so tired of the lies and the games. Time after time, he was going out with what he called "his buddies."

I was so emotionally traumatized that I began thinking and sinking into a deep, dark hole of hopelessness and depression. I took pills and more pills. I ran out in front of cars, hoping they would hit and kill me. Other suicidal thoughts ran through my mind as I was trying to get rid of the pain. I always thought we'd be together happily ever after. This shattered my dreams of marriage. I was crushed and felt I had lost my identity. What would I do now, who would I be, what would become of me? I wanted to leave, but I thought I needed to try harder. I got pregnant twice so we could have a baby boy. I thought (surely) he'd love me now. I was so happy that I was pregnant. I was going to be a mother for the second and third time, and it was a boy. My husband looked at me and said our budget cannot handle another baby. This left me feeling like I was not a worthy wife because I didn't meet my or other people's expectations. My thoughts were bouncing back and forth out of control.

When I was a child, I always knew my parents loved me. Still, they always treated me as though something was wrong with me. I had many child psychiatry visits, and my stomach constantly hurt. I was always going to the doctor or the hospital. Experiencing molestation as a child led to rape. I held all these thoughts and feelings in my heart, never telling anyone until years later that the things I've experienced, such as problems in school, only made me feel they were right. I rushed to get married, got pregnant, and had a miscarriage. Through all my pain points, the abuse of disrespect continued.

Being called the B word and then expecting me to have sex with him after mistreating me did not make sense. This seemed to be what they call the crazy cycle in marriage counseling. In the crazy cycle, nothing makes sense! Everybody's arguing and making decisions without one another and not communicating properly.

I think our budget can't handle another baby. Still, you can smoke weed, and you can drink and spend money on women. I remember he flew to Washington with this woman to meet her parents as if he was about to get married again. He was still married to me. I'm still here going through the same crazy cycle (problems) that doesn't make any sense. That's the crazy cycle. I felt like my brain was going to explode with anger, jealousy, and other harmful thoughts that plagued my mind.

I know you're thinking you went to marriage counseling. Yes, we did, and the cheating continued, validating more worthlessness. I thought to myself, why can't I do anything right? One devastating blow after the other. My life was like someone was constantly beating the life out of me. I FELT I wasn't worthy enough to live, and I contemplated committing suicide.

I Prayed and Said, God, If You Are Real, Help Me and Heal Me from This Crazy perverted love cycle. Lord, I need you to help me. I'm losing my mind. I do not want to live this way! I cried out to the Lord for his mercy, love, and help. I could see lights in the direction that I would follow. The direction was to divorce my husband and begin to meditate on the word of God.

He helped me find my identity so I wouldn't waste my life or time. God gave me a precious gift called a divine purpose. I knew that by telling my story and helping other women become free from what I call the crazy cycle, there was hope for the hopeless. Romans 10:13 KJV – "For whosoever shall call on the name of the Lord shall be saved." Saved means to be delivered and saved from whatever you need to be saved or delivered from.

God wants a relationship with his children. He created us for his glory; every story would give Him glory for how He's helped us walk victoriously. To live a life of joy and peace and to have the right state of mind. Raise your children right in fear of the Lord and watch them become successful along with you and me. Proverbs 23:7 (KJV) – "As a man thinks in his heart, so is he." You and I must always guard our thoughts and hearts, paying close attention to what's in them. You want to get to where everything you say, agreeing with everything that is genuinely wholesome in your thoughts, will not harm you or your family. Because as you think, so you and I become.

I was in an extremely dark place in my life, muttering over and over, meditating on what a failure I'd been. I often thought about being a failure when I watched the news or read the newspapers. Back in the day, they would talk about premeditated murder. I never realized this was leading to premeditation to take my own life, suicide. I was meditating and soaking in every problem, every situation, and everything that had ever happened to me. My thoughts were blocking and preventing me from seeing that there was hope for a brighter future.

And what you (think) or meditate on will come to pass, good or bad. Joshua 1:8 KJV – "This book of the law shall not depart out of thy mouth, but thou shalt meditate therein day and night, that thou mayest observe to do according to all that is written therein; for then thou shall make thy way prosperous, and then thou shall have good success." Joshua 1:9 KJV – "Have not I commanded thee? Be strong and of good courage; be not afraid, neither be dismayed: for the Lord thy God is with you whithersoever thou go."

So, what we think is very, very important. We must be around positive people full of faith, vision, purpose, and goals to help us see life better. You will become what you think. This is how you find your identity. We will bloom and growwwwwww by developing the right mindset that will shape us in our Purpose, Character, and Integrity, showing strengths and weaknesses that will teach us life lessons along the way. We have assistance so that we may conquer pain and failure instead of letting them destroy us and turn our pain and failure into purposeful, enduring, faith-filled experiences that teach us never to give up, always turning problems into opportunities and opportunities into success stories. Just like all the amazing coauthors in this awesome book!

Faith in the spiritual world is like money in the natural world. When you have enough, you can achieve any success that aligns with God's plan. Luke 1:37 KJV "For with God nothing [is or ever] shall be impossible." We will never achieve success until we've experienced failure, rejection, or loss. The invitation of what your enemies have said or done to you does not matter. Don't listen to the Naysayers, the Wanna Doers, the Gonna Doers, and the Never Doers.

The Never Doers say you will never make it, you're not smart enough, you don't have what it takes, you will never be successful, and you'll never be married to the right person. You will never get healed. You will never have kids. You will never fulfill all your dreams and goals. You are never going to write that book. You will never win an Emmy Award for that song. You will never start that business and be successful. You will never be a billionaire. I'm having a little fun, which is the opposite of what that negative group says. I'm going to do it. I'm going to the next level.

Light afflictions 2 Corinthians 4:17 KJV – "For our light affliction, which is for the moment, worketh for us more and more exceedingly an eternal weight of glory." Light afflictions are not the general problems humans go through; it is the discipline, discomfort, and contentment we are willing to endure for the sake of Christ. When we view our problems as momentary and not a lifestyle, we can see that we are problem solvers looking at failure and pain.

Knowing failure isn't final; we become stronger, wiser, and better. Pain is only temporary, and "ROYALTY IS FOREVER" when we deal with THE PRINCE OF PEACE. We can find our true identity in our

Royal Covenant that was given to you and me when Jesus died on Calvary. 2 Peter 1:3 KJV – God's "According as His Divine power hath given us everything that pertains to Life and Godliness." That means nothing is missing, lacking, or broken, and we can access everything we need with the faith that He's given us. With our "ROYAL IDENTITY," we are Real Kings and Queens Reigning in Authority. He said in Genesis, the beginning of the Bible, take dominion. We are to take dominion over anything that gets out of order, not people but the demonic spirits that operate THROUGH them and do Victorious Warfare with Our Prayers.

As we continue to press forward toward our life achievements, there will be doubts, fears, and distractions. We must stay focused; don't let doubt drown our dreams. Thinking the economy is too slow, I don't know if my business or relationship will survive. GOD has uniquely made us in his image Genesis 1:26-27 - KJV, And God said, "Let us (Father, Son, Holy Spirit) make man in Our image, according to Our likeness [not physical, but a spiritual personality and moral likeness]; and let them have complete authority over the fish of the sea, the birds of the air, the cattle, and over the entire earth, and over everything that creeps and crawls on the earth." "So, God created man in His (own) image, in the image and likeness of God He created him; male and female He created them."

WE ALL are uniquely made and equipped for success. Everyone has a gift, according to Ephesians 4:7-8. "Yet Grace (Undeserved Favor) was given to each one of us (not indiscriminately, but in different ways) in proportion to the measure of Christ's (rich and abundant) gifts. Therefore, it says: ***"When he ascended on high, he led captivity captive, and he bestowed gifts on men."***

How anyone moves from failure to enduring faith is by faith. We were created as believers. Whether you believe in God or not, you always think positively or negatively. You will feel you are going to make it, or you think you're not going to make it. You still believe that no matter what was said or done, you let your haters be your motivators, and you will move from failure to success!

We can overcome and be great if we walk by the guidelines of God's wisdom. Genesis 12:1 says, "Go away from your country and from your relatives and from your father's house to the land which I will show you, and I will make you a great nation, and I will bless you [abundantly], and make your name great [exalted, distinguished]; and you shall be a blessing [a source of great good to others]; and I will bless (do good for, benefit) those who bless you, and I will curse [that is subject to My wrath and judgment] the one who curses (despises, dishonors, has contempt for) you. And in you, all the families (nations) of the earth will be blessed." God is saying I will bless those who bless you and curse them who curse you. So many people, even in the church, don't realize they've already been blessed. We must learn to walk by faith into our blessings with our gifts, talents, and abilities and stop acting like we've been cursed.

Take an example of a caterpillar and how they start as worms. They don't look like they're equipped to fly and become something more, something beautiful, something adored, something full of color. It's much more than what it looks like in the beginning, and in the right season, it turns into a beautiful butterfly. The butterfly is free to be what they were created to be. It's just like us. We look like we may be crawling on our bellies with doubt, fear, unbelief, death, oppression, depression, lacking skills and abilities.

As we yield to God's will, everything that we were equipped for, meaning everything we need to succeed, is in you and me. Pain births fourth purpose because if we were not challenged, we would be lazy. We would not search to find all the hidden treasures, gifts, talents, and abilities in life. They are inside us, so we become winners when we see our purpose in our pain. We become successful. Doubt is a feeling of fear, and dreams are a series of thoughts. Anything is always possible if we believe.

Acknowledge what you know. Jude 1:23 shows mercy; if you are holding out, you are holding back from others. Your gifts are for sharing and making them a priority is what you should be spending most of your time on. If your priority is God, then your blessings will flow! And you will be fulfilled serving others. That's a given, you know.

I learned a lot of lessons concerning failure not being final. I realized I could always get back up again and become stronger, more significant, and wiser. I can love again, and thank God I did. God healed my heart and mind and blessed me with an Awesome King named Harold Ward Britton Sr. We are coming up on 29 years of marriage.

After that first marriage, I thought I'd never love or marry again. I am learning that God does miraculous miracles and helps us through our problems. Failure isn't final, but it leads us down the road of life, which is a phenomenal find. I would have never known that I could love again if I hadn't failed at that first marriage and found true love and turned it into a miracle.

My husband is handsome, kind, fun-loving, and an incredible man of God. He loves me like his Queen and our ten children as Royal Princes and Princesses. Life and marriage are a journey. I learned not to be unequally yoked regarding your soul mate. This means having God first in your life and having a lot in common with each other. Understanding one another's likes and dislikes, and don't forget NOT to push each other's buttons, lol, you know what I mean.

As my husband and I enjoyed time together, we (both) overcame divorces but were doing very well. Then, I was attacked with a lung disease from inhaling all the toxic chemicals from inside the GM plant. I had thirteen specialists who said I had dementia toxics in all my vital organs. I was on thirteen medications. The doctors said I would be on those medications for the rest of my life. I was on an asthma pump daily and a pump whenever I had severe asthma attacks. I learned very well how to speak the word of God over my situation and disease, realizing my authority as a Real Royal Queen. I rebuke death at times when I had severe breathing problems.

Declaring I will Live and not die, but I will live and declare the goodness of the Lord by His stripes, I AM HEALED. I had a horrible cough, but I continued to stand in faith. I AM Whole! I constantly coughed up spittle saliva that was yellow, black, and white. I was choking a lot to clear my Airways so I could breathe. The doctor told me within two years, I would be in a wheelchair, and after that, the lung disease would consume me, and there would be no more me. That's another reason why you want to develop your faith. As much faith as you can create by speaking the word of God over your situation, you gain more trust and confidence in whatever happens in life. You will overcome it. As I said, faith in the spiritual world is like money in the natural world, and you can have what you say. Matthew tells us we can speak to the mountains, and they must obey/move, so whatever problem you have, remember you are royalty!!! Live a life of abundance and blessings that align with God's word and his will/divine plans. It has your name on it.

Never be denied anything that you want. Those things that align with God's word will afford you anything and everything you need, from the natural world into the spiritual world and back. Within seven months, I was completely healed. Noted by the doctors, they were amazed because they thought I would be sick for the rest of my life. Another battle was won for the Royal benefit of being a daughter of the KING. 1 Peter 2:9, you are of the Royal Priesthood-Priesthood is a Royal family comprised of Kings, Queens, Princes, and Princesses. This is where we draw our Royal Identity and authority from. My Royal Identity defines me as unique, powerful, beautiful, intelligent, and gracious.

I am blessed, I am prosperous, I am strong, I am healthy, I am talented, I am creative, I am confident, I am secure, I am disciplined, I am focused, I am attractive, and I am well-liked. I have a great personality, and I believe the right people will be in my future. The right opportunities are headed my way. I will accomplish all my dreams, and I will overcome every obstacle. 2024/25 are my years! Things have shifted in my favor. God is about to show me something that I've never seen. It's going to be bigger, better, and greater. I've never imagined that I would be in shape (I am), weigh what I'm supposed to (I do), and be redeemed by the Lord. So, I say (today), in Jesus' name, Amen and Amen.

My King, My Husband, My Pastor, and I, Pastor of The Royal Priesthood Ministries Church 2518 Delaware Ave. Flint, MI 48506. We are also building a billion-dollar business with Sir Dr. James Dentley and Queen Lynette in the TLC business. My King is building a billion-dollar business with Lincoln Heritage Insurance Company to serve God and his people in whatever global capacity we can—for example, education identity distribution centers, food banks, and water well centers. I give God all the glory for bringing us this far. I know we will finish our assignments, and we will finish them strong. I am a Song Artist. I have a Song: I Am Blessed to the Max.

I am not taking it back, but together, we'll take over and serve everyone we can and bless them by helping them fulfill their goals, dreams, and visions. Thank you for reading my story, blessings.

NOTE: *The spiritual quotes within this chapter have come from the spiritual text. Some are exact, and some are paraphrased to some degree.*

About The Author

Sherri Britton

Sherri L. Britton, Queen of Royalty, was born in Flint, Michigan, in 1957. She has been married for 29 years to her King, Harold Britton. They have ten children, seventy grandchildren, and three great-grandchildren. She is a music artist who produced one CD, "I Am Blessed 2 The Max."

Her Biblical/Spiritual Journey:

Sherri is also a Children's Teacher for the (BFS) Bible Fellowship Study International. She speaks at many conferences and community events on many different subject matters in the spiritual arena. Sherri loves to help and serve others by educating people in holistic and spiritual health seminars in Flint, Michigan.

Her Vision:

Sherri empowers women, elevates generations, and unleashes their REAL IDENTITY to find their Purpose and Potential and shift their mindset from ordinary to extraordinary Royalty Queens.

Her Mission:

To empower women to reveal their true identity as a Royal Queen and Ignite the fire of their God-given purpose to strive for a Greater Spiritual Dimension. To continue imparting a new mindset with the word of God while recognizing the capabilities of her gifts, talents, and abilities that will birth integrity and godly character. To enhance financial stability, and finally, natural beauty that shines with her charm because she is a whole person in Christ. With great confidence, she knows she is a Royal Queen.

Harold Britton – Pastor

Sherri Britton – Co-Pastor
Royal Priesthood Ministries Church
2518 Delaware, Ave, Flint, Michigan 48506

10

There Is A Spirit In Now

Cynthia Morson

"There is a spirit in now. There is a spirit - The spirit of God in man. No man is devoid of it. Most of us are as unaware of it as we are of the blood coursing through our bodies. God is with us. God's presence feels all space. The Spirit of God dwells in us. But how many people have felt that presence? Talked about, prayed about, theorized about, and sermonized about the spirit of God. But it is not experienced. It is the conscious awareness that actual feeling or realization of the presence is necessary."

–Joel Goldsmith

Thank you, God, for allowing me to feel complete in every moment. You've created me perfect, whole, and complete on a soulful level. You touched me to feel your spirit in every aspect of my life to my core.

I'm already home. I never had to feel like that: "We live and move and have our being in God."

"I'm already home," so I meditated on those words. In those moments, I discovered how we project our attention outward. The list includes stories, words, experiences, ideas, judgments, criticisms, anxieties, hurts, etc. The focus takes us away from this moment, the now.

I made my point when I reached for the book "YOU CAN HEAL YOUR LIFE" by Louise Hay. In her book, she shares different ways to use (what I call) her 'transformational journey of change. This list can be referred to when you have issues or problems. The idea is to list (on paper) the physical problem, the cause of the problem, and the new thought pattern needed to move forward.

I will share my real-life challenge as your example.

My **Problem:** Stroke (Cerebrovascular Accident/CVA).

My **Challenge:** Probable Cause: Giving Up. Resistance. "Rather die than change—rejection of life."

My **New Thought Pattern**: Life is Changing! I must adapt quickly to the new. I accept life's past, present, and future.

This example came from Louise L. Hay. However, I listed my true-life example to share my challenges, struggles, pain points, and the will to transform from darkness into the light of healing, going, and growing. It's not what happens to you; how you respond to it matters!

Already at Home – There's No Place Like Home!

In The Wizard of Oz, Dorothy is sleeping and shows seven adventures of a little girl who lost her way back home. She meets several characters, the point being, "When she was finally on her way home, she was told to close her eyes. And she repeated." There's no place like home, over and over and over. A picture appeared of Dorothy at home, lying in her bed, dreaming. "How often do we find ourselves at home?"

Who do you see when you look in the mirror of your soul?

Do you recognize the image? We ask ourselves or avoid asking ourselves, who is that person staring back at me in the mirror? Where is the person you've known all your life? Was the journey meaningful?

What happened to me? What does it take to get on with life? This is not who I am, and this is not where I am supposed to be. Welcome to the adventure of being me. SOUL!

Words have power and inspiration for the many daily challenges, illnesses, and harmful effects of seeing life through limiting beliefs are available. Present circumstances are the veil of illusion. Address feelings of lack, destructive relationships, and non-loving feelings for self, friends, family, and partners. To provide an outlet that supports releasing and clearing negative thoughts and choosing more abundant, healthy, and loving thoughts. Here are several short affirmations that keep me going.

I am not limited by past challenges.
I can be, do, and have my heart desires.
I'm a winner, and nobody can steal my dream.
I choose my thoughts with love.
I constantly have new insights and new ways of looking at my world.
I am willing to change and grow.
What is the greatest weakness of man... not to believe?
My Inner Being is Electrified with Perpetual Health (Linda Wilks).
I Am a Radiator to God's Divine Light (Linda Wilks).
I Can Afford Anything.
I Radiate God's Power in Every Cell in My Body.
I Am the Beloved Thinking.

I was married to Derrick Jones, and we had two daughters, Kizzie-Shavon and TaKara-Krystal. We lived in Portland, Oregon, and we had a good time. Derrick worked for Standard Steel, Pepsi-Cola, and the Koin Companies. They were excellent jobs and paid well. But he liked to take drugs. Today, we share our granddaughter's likes because we are friends.

I went to Northwestern Community Church and was a choir member. I was also selected to be a Praise and Worship Leader. I was also assigned to be a (HIM) Home-Involved Minister. The Minister would give us church lessons after Church. I had about twenty people come to my home.

It was beautiful seeing people from the Church. A lady asked me to pray for her to receive the Holy Spirit. I prayed, and she received the Holy Spirit. *I Loved the Happiness of Life in The Conviction That We Had.*

My father picked me and my daughters up from the bus. I looked out of the window, and I could feel my destiny. It was like it was calling me. When I look at the buildings, they look so close, yet so far. I needed to get a job and take care of my daughters. It didn't come without heartache, but it was not easy. I had a job and an apartment and lived on my own.

My daughter was in second grade, and I told her she was in school to learn. I talked to her, and she listened. When I told her to go to school, she had better listen. But she wanted to do good because she knew she would get flowers and money when she passed. And she was a success. Krystal was different; she loved to read. But this year was a new school year. When she got home, I wondered what happened because she was crying, as if someone had broken her heart. I had to go to school and report that the reading book was outdated. She brought home new, updated reading material from school the next day.

The Following is Dear to My Heart:

Today, I have a deeper thought for these words. I am a master, and I give myself permission to succeed. I make critical decisions quickly and decisively. I am a master. I react promptly to critical decisions without emotion or hesitation. I am a masterful listener and consult my higher self to find a solution before speaking or responding.

Is Your Destiny Calling You?

Destiny is powerful, energetic, ancient, soul-based, and demanding. Destiny is the tension of your soul beckoning you toward fulfilling your dreams. It is the whispering that awakens you at three a.m. It is the yearning that you may not quite grasp and don't yet understand. It is something somewhere calling you from beyond your current place. It is ultimately the answer to your deepest, most profound questions. The call of your destiny will not leave you alone.

Over 10,000 years ago, the wise yogis of India and profound sages of Greece believed that a person has only two desires. The same belief is true today. But what two desires could satiate?

All human longing? It is not health, power, money, or even love - it is much simpler than that. Humans are truly happy with a peaceful mind and a joyful heart. In fact, this is your destiny, the ultimate destiny of every human being.

"You are the Master of the Moments of Your Life" – *By Paramahamsa Yogananda*

Destiny is not a new age, modern-day, self-help personality concept. It is not trendy, static, wimpy, ethereal, or powerless. It is not something or someone that judges or is self-righteous. It favors no one - not the rich, poor, educated, non-educated, sick, healthy, famous, or unknown. Because destiny recognizes that everyone is a soul first and a human being second, it honors the path of all living beings.

> "You are what your deep, driving desire is.
> As your deep, driving desire is, so is your will.
> As your deed is, so is your deed.
> As your deed is, so is your destiny."
>
> ***Upanishads***

As for health, many people in America believe health is the absence of disease. This is not true. Health is having the vitality and vibrancy to do what you want to at any given moment of your everyday life. In its infinite wisdom, the body desires to have high energy levels. This requires a balance of rest and activity, nutritious eating, exercising daily, and perhaps most importantly, loving the body you have by sending it positive affirmations.

I was born into a religious family. We attended Church every Sunday. I had four brothers and one sister. Some people attended Church the whole day, from Sunday school to late-night singing. Dad had a group, the Kingdom Group Singers. I could not wait to leave home and stop attending Church.

Thoughts create, and they ought to be loved.

Thinking back to my third year of high school. I started hanging out with girls who didn't attend high school. I had perfect grades my whole school career. But this year, I want to be with these girls. I wasn't smoking or drinking. Just being with them was cool. I recall the day we went over to this house. One by one, the girls went into this room. Then it was my turn. Several boys tried to have sex with me. I fought for my life. I was kicking and fighting with both arms. They left me alone. I was scared and nervous as I ran out of that house as fast as I could.

But the next day at school, I sensed something was wrong. They didn't like me anymore. I guess because I didn't do what they did. The eight girls chased me home. They wanted to beat me up. I ran home alone. I only had two friends before that group of eight girls. I never believed in anyone as my friend since then. Vicky liked to drink like a grown-up. The following two years of seeing those guys, they greeted me with much respect.

I was confused when I left home to go to college. I had no adult friends. I never had a conversation that made me feel like I was okay. I was so insecure. Even though I had eight to nine aunts and almost the same number of uncles, no one ever said, "Hi Cynthia, how do you feel?"

My brother, whom I loved, was sneaking around in the dark, entering my bedroom. He was getting on top of me like I was his girlfriend. I felt something down there, but I was scared to say something. It happened several times. Each time, my brother never uttered a word until high school. We carried on during the day like it never happened. This was a traumatizing experience having my brother come into my room at night, get in my bed, and get on top of me. I must have been in shock at what was happening, and my reaction was not to fight or flight but to freeze and not say anything. Fear is a powerful weapon.

I wanted to be a flight attendant when I finished high school, but I was too young. So, they told my Dad and the Assistant Principal, Mr. Heinz. He arranged for me to go to Ellsworth Community College, an all-white town. My experience orientation experience at Ellsworth Community College in Iowa Falls, Iowa, was horrible. No one asked me about me when I returned home for school breaks and holidays. I was so insecure. I always felt people were talking about me behind my back.

About eighty black guys were attending college, and they all played sports. All the guys liked me, Cynthia. My mind quickly flashed back to my mistrust of my brothers and father, and I did not trust my male college students because of my past experiences. I made it through the first year intact; no incidents or male drama existed. But in my second year, I met Kevin Anderson. We were hot and heavy, like two peas in a pot.

Kevin visited me at my parents' house, and I got caught in bed with him. Shit, that was a horrible experience. He got kicked out of my parents' house, and I was not allowed to visit him in his hotel room. When I returned to school after Christmas break, Kevin had a ring for me and asked me to marry him. So, I did. I got pregnant and decided against the baby. I didn't have love for anything. I didn't realize that I was mentally, physically, and psychologically abused because of my brother's actions when he used to violate me in my room at night when we were in high school.

Here is another part of My Life, My Story, that, today, and for the rest of my life, I have ongoing daily challenges to deal with. There are visible and hidden disabilities that millions of people have. ***Please pay close attention to my story from here on.*** I will say that people who see me don't see my disability on the outside. However, when you hear me talking, you can listen to the effects and challenges that my hidden disability has caused me.

Now, allow me to share my story about what happened to me.

I was going to Bali's fitness workout club because my girlfriend invited me. I was driving Uber in my car when I suddenly noticed something was a little bit off. My words were repeating, over and over. This never happened to me before, and I began to get nervous and uncomfortable because I was driving alone.

I called Linda, and she and her family were going to the movies. They wanted me to go with them, but I felt weird and did not understand what was happening. I told Linda I was not my usual self and thought I should go home. Linda agreed. I noticed I was repeating my words over and over. I began sounding weird. I told Linda no! I thought going home was best.

I called Mariam, and she asked me how I was doing. Mariam told me that I sounded like I was having a stroke. I sounded like I was driving, and she said she could tell by how I was talking that I was having a stroke. Then we lost our cell connection, and the phone died.

I continued driving and stopped at a store. I jumped out of the car and went in. I was in the store for about three minutes before I immediately walked out, returned to my car, and drove off, but nothing happened. I was saved and made it home - at least, that's what I was thinking!

My daughter was home, and I told her I wanted to go to bed. I did not tell her something was wrong with me. I told her I was okay. I woke up, and I did not feel good and found myself wanting to go to the hospital. I told my daughter, and she called an ambulance. The ambulance arrived, and the paramedics checked me out, asking several questions about what was happening to me. They strapped me to the gurney and transported me to the hospital. I remember hearing the loud noise from the sirens as the driver made his way through traffic. The next thing I knew, I found myself at Oak Park Hospital. A five-minute ride seemed like it took hours. Once I arrived, I was in the waiting room to be admitted. For whatever reason, I don't remember why I was not admitted. Without any explanation, I was transported to Rush Hospital on the West Side of Chicago.

I Was Admitted, And Oh, I Was Scared To Death. I didn't have any information about what my condition was, what was going on, or the reason I was not admitted to Oak Park Hospital. I was taken to a ward that didn't look friendly. I went past two male nurses while being taken to a room, and I was scared and left alone. I slept with my clothes on, and I woke up three or four times that night wondering what was happening to me.

The following day, I was given breakfast. I still didn't understand what was going on. It was a nightmare. When the doctor called in, I didn't understand what he was saying. I went to a routine stroke patients' unit. I was in physical therapy while praying for a speedy recovery. I was locked down all the time I was there. I had to tell the hospital staff when I went to use the bathroom and when I showered. All the time, doctors are coming into my room. I didn't understand. I was clueless. I was given exercises to do while standing. This was to check my balance and ensure I would not fall while walking or standing during regular periods.

It was around Christmas time, and Kizzie and TaKara made things right for me. Every day, Linda called to talk with me. I had to stay in the hospital, and I still wasn't ready or allowed to be discharged.

I had to go to another hospital ward for medicine. It took the doctors overnight before I was discharged. I take Hydrochlorothiazide now for the Nifedipine. I went to Kizzie and Jason's house and stayed for seven months. They lived in Elgin, Illinois, a Northwest Suburb of Chicago. I stayed with TaKara and Bioko on the weekends.

I enrolled in the Aetna Hospital Day Rehabilitation Program, which was very convenient. I had physical and speech therapy three times a week. The muscles in my legs were tested and evaluated to see if I had damage to my muscular system. The upper muscular system was fine. I had to exercise my upper body using a workout program. I also used a home radial finger workout with a ball squeeze and isolated finger extensions.

The speech therapy professional started by instructing me to verbally recite my name, address, birth date, month, and year. The speech professional began with who and action verbs over the next several weeks. One of the most challenging things for me was to hear something and then write it. That was the matching and identification process, and it was hard. I know I was starting from baby lessons. This was the hardest thing for me to do, and I had to force myself to make time to do it. Function language, answering questions, and vocabulary were all part of rebuilding. One of the symptoms of my stroke was that I suffered from Aphasia, which is an acquired language disorder often resulting from a stroke (which I had) or a brain injury. Aphasia can affect language, speaking, listening, reading, and writing. And I had all the symptoms. I had Aphasia treatments on 1/16/23 (56.7|100 moderate). On 3/14/23 (83.8|100), on 3/23/23 (86.2|100), and again on 7/26/23 (91.6|100).

Aphasia is something I learned to live with. Think about what you want to say before you say it. I had to adjust to using facial expressions, gestures, and pointing to convey my ideas. I also had to start drawing and writing keywords to improve my communication skills. If I can't think of a word, describe it, or use a similar word, I must figure out the best methods to get my message out. I had to eliminate distractions and look for my communication partner. Remember: Aphasia is a loss of language, not intellect!

This was a very traumatic journey. However, I was, and still am, determined to be a productive contributor to society. That is one of the many reasons for sharing my story within the pages of this book – My Life My Story! If I can do it, so can you. Remember, any excuse is a reason to fail. I did not allow my stroke to be my excuse for failure. Yes, it is a temporary setback. However, it is not a failure. Back to my story!

While I stayed with Kizzie, sometimes I had to cry. I felt like there was something wrong with me. I cried, felt sorry for myself, worried, anxious, or troubled about my future. I was disturbed by walking down the stairs. I talk strangely at times. The simple, everyday things we take for granted were now hard for me to navigate through because of my stroke.

I was in fear of having another stroke. I felt anger and grief about the things I'd lost. I was in shock and felt helplessness, which are all-natural emotions after experiencing a stroke. Coping with these emotions is not easy. If you feel anxious or low, speak to someone about your feelings. You do not need to suffer in silence. Like me, there is help available for you.

I had a friend who lived in California pray for me. My friend prayed for me three different times. The first time my friend prayed for me, I burned a candle and lit incense. She even prayed for my daughter. I slept a while, and she called two times to see if I woke up. She prayed. And she was so glad for the few words I spoke. I was making progress as her prayers were being answered.

How can you obtain a life filled with peace, love, joy, and harmony without focusing on the material necessities?

Jesus tells us how:

"But seek first the kingdom of God and His righteousness, and all these things shall be added unto you." – (ESV) Matthew 6:33.

We are told to have God's righteousness or right-mindedness and develop the right thought pattern. Develop the correct thinking governed by intelligence that is positive, not negative, unselfish, not self-centered, creative, not destructive, and kind and not hateful. Employ this attitude, and everything you need for a good life will multiply.

Today, as I am writing this short narrative about My Life My Story, I reflect on (ESV) Psalm 23:1 – 4: "Yea, though I walked through the valley of the shadow of death, I will fear no evil; for thou art with me; thy rod and thy staff comfort me."

What this means to me is that during and after my stroke, I stated that I WAS SCARED TO DEATH. At that time, I was. However, as time moved on, and my family and friends stayed by my side, with the medical services, rehabilitation, and visits after visits for different therapy sessions, I began to get better and better. I am not like I used to be. However, I am better than ever. My family, friends, faith, trust, and belief in God pulled me through.

I can talk, I can walk, I can drive by myself, and I can do everything I did before having my stroke. Even though some things are still challenging, I did not quit and allowed my temporary setback to become a permanent failure.

I am one of many participants in a documentary. Remember I told you that I suffered from Aphasia because of my stroke? Aphasia can affect language, speaking, listening, reading, and writing. And I had all the symptoms. Writing this chapter and filming my session were challenging. During the filming, we prayed before we started the session.

At first, I was a little nervous because of my Aphasia. But once I got comfortable, I answered the questions as best I could. We took a few short breaks because the cameraman (James Barnes) and the interviewer (Michael Bart Mathews) noticed I was becoming emotional during my session. They made me feel comfortable before we continued with the session. I was proud of that accomplishment because Aphasia does not affect intelligence. All of my thought power is still intact. I now must think about what I want and how to say certain things to get my message out.

At the end of the session, I felt relieved that I was brave enough to face my fear and not allow fear to stop me from shining my light. I was the first person interviewed that day, and I did not have the opportunity to watch or learn from someone who went before me. But I did it! I became a leader that day because I was the pacesetter. Ninety percent of success is showing up. I feel blessed to have shown up on that faithful day.

I have two incredible daughters and a new grandbaby. I attended the Inspired2Speak speakers camp under the coaching of Sir Dr. James Dentley and his team of servant leaders. Being in this environment has helped me (to continue to) find my voice and share it with the masses. I hope and pray that My Life My Story has shed an illuminating light on your journey in life. We all are fearfully and wonderfully made (NIV), Psalm 139:14, paraphrased. Let me break it down for you. Fearfully means great reverence, heartfelt interest, and respect.

We all have unique challenges, trials, tribulations, setbacks, roadblocks, forks in the road, and sometimes dead ends. We must become like the eagle and fly high enough that the hawk cannot breathe. Then you know you are associating with other eagles who have your best interest. My eagles stayed with me throughout my recovery and are still with me. I am blessed to have this opportunity to help and serve others by sharing My Life My Story in this amazing book.

About The Author

Cynthia Morson

Cynthia Morson has an extensive list of educational and professional achievements:

- Health Services Investigator I: 01/1989 to 01/2014.
- Home Involve Minister (HIM), Northwestern Christian Church, Portland, Oregon, Rev. James Roper Paster: May 2004.
- Practitioner of Religious Science: March 5, 2005.
- Board of Directors of Religious Science International: May 5, 2005.
- Licensed as a Minister of Religious Science: May 15, 2007.
- Certified Master Coach of Neuro-Linguistic Programming - Master Practitioner of Neuro-Linguistic Programming, Master Hypnotist Certification - Master Practitioner Timeline Therapy: July 1, 2018.
- Life Coaching Certification: January 2, 2019.
- Life Coaching Certification: How to Start a Business Life Coaching online: Feb 2019.

- Living, Breathing Blueprint for your Purpose, Passion, Vision, and Plan: March 16, 2019.
- Certificate Yoga Trainer: December 19, 2019.
- Certificate of Graduation: Digital Marketing/Workshop for Woman Entrepreneurs: August 12, 2020.
- Certificate of completion - Clinical Hypnotherapy: June 13, 2021.
- Successfully completed 2-day, in-person Quantum-Touch Level I training: June 27, 21.
- Certified Transformative Coach Practitioner: August 20, 2021.
- Certified Practitioner of Geo Love Healing: December 12, 2021.
- Certified Speaker/INSPIRED2SPEAK: April 5-7, 2024, by Sir Dr. James Dentley.

11

Rise Above Adversity

Sabrina Clayton

I am no stranger to adversity. Now, I'm not going to tell you that I was raised in the hood, surrounded by drugs, alcohol, and street violence on every corner. No, that's not my story! At least not in my younger childhood years. As a young child, I was raised with all the conveniences in life. I grew up in a two-parent home with a strong father figure who owned and operated a construction company and later opened a local business in the community. My mother was a stay-at-home mom who kept our home clean and our bellies full of her good cooking! We had a good life, even though Mom and Dad were sometimes too strict and overprotective.

We enjoyed new clothes and shoes every year and went to the best schools. My dad took the family to Disney World every summer—life was amazing! It wasn't until later, from middle school through high school, that I learned about life's hard knocks. Our seemingly perfect family wasn't so perfect anymore. My parents started having trouble in their marriage, separated, and then eventually divorced. Financially and emotionally, the struggle became real for all of us.

My mother was suddenly a divorced parent with four children to support, and she had to learn how to depend mainly on her income to make ends meet. I remember this was the first time in my life that I heard my mother say, "No, I can't afford that." I remember thinking at that time, with my entitled young mind, "What do you mean, no?" My mind could not comprehend the enormity of their divorce and how it would affect my lifestyle going forward.

I was too young and selfish to be concerned about how this change would affect my mother's lifestyle, her broken heart, or my siblings. If I wanted to buy something my mother thought was too expensive, I would have to ask my dad, or I would have to learn how to live without it.

I was about to embark on a new journey through high school and then on to college, appreciating the many sacrifices that my mother had made for us. My dad was still present with financial support, but not emotionally or physically. It was also a time in my young life when I had to learn how to practice gratitude and humility. My mother was instrumental in teaching us the importance of being grateful for our many blessings, regardless of our circumstances at the time.

In a couple of years, we went from a lifestyle of the haves to the have-nots. We had to learn how to appreciate the positive aspects of our lives and practice gratitude for the things we did have and not what we didn't have. Adversity and life challenges started showing up in our lives, and we had to learn a new way to navigate them. Rising above adversity in life can be a challenging but rewarding process. Adversity (is defined as) a very difficult, unfavorable situation, hardship, or misfortune.

Soon after my parents separated, my mother found a low-income three-bedroom apartment for us to live in. We moved from our comfortable, larger single-family home in the suburbs into the ghetto. This was quite an adjustment for me, my mother, and my siblings. This was a new neighborhood, which introduced another challenge for me. Like I said in the beginning, I don't remember being surrounded by drugs, alcohol, and street violence on every corner. Still, I do remember some neighborhood kids smoking reefer, aka marijuana, sometimes. That was the extent of my exposure since we weren't allowed to hang out in the streets.

About a year after moving there, I had my first bullying experience. My bully was taller and bigger than me. I was a thin-sized girl but strong. She was thicker and much stronger. She was a smart bully because she would never bother me in school or on the school bus. She would wait until we were off the bus and walking home. After all, she didn't want to risk being kicked out of school or off the bus. She made sure that the only witnesses would be the neighborhood kids.

I remember one day, she increased her level of harassment and recruited a few friends to join her cause. She was the ringleader with a gang of girlfriends walking behind me and hazing me. They would kick dirt on me, throw rocks, call me names, and even push me a couple of times, but I would keep on walking. They tried everything they could to break me down, but I would not break. I kept repeating, "Sticks and stones may break my bones, but words will never hurt me."

I didn't know it then, but I had already formed a resilient mind during those challenging moments. The hazing, pushing, and name-calling continued for days. I never told my mother for fear of being embarrassed by her talking to the bully's mother. God forbid! Besides, I thought that would make matters worse. So, I continued to take it day after day. Turn the other cheek, right? Right. One day, both sides of my cheeks were bruised, and I had enough! Enough of the dirt and the rocks! Enough of the kicks, the tripping, and pushing! Enough of the abuse!

The next day was the day that I snapped. I was being hazed and ridiculed again by my bully and her posse, who followed me (all the way) to my apartment door. I can hear them heckling and spewing verbal assaults behind my back. I stepped in front of my door with my keys shaking in my hand, trembling while opening the lock. As soon as I opened my door, someone pushed my bully into me, and we both fell into the entrance of my home onto the floor! I was so scared yet angry at the same time because I thought she was attacking me in my own home!

I do not know where my sudden strength came from, but somehow, I was able to push her off me and started punching with all my might! I remember pulling her hair and beating her! It must have been a burst of adrenaline from my fear that kicked in at that moment because it took several girls to pull me off her. It was my moment to fight or flight! I had decided to fight this time - I had enough!

While several girls held me back, I saw my mom run into the living room, yelling, "What is going on here? What are you all doing?" She realized it must have been a fight because my hair and clothes were a mess. My books were thrown all over the floor, and about six girls were standing near the entrance of our front door. They all quickly left my house once they heard my mother coming. Of course, the bully, her sister, and most of her friends had fled the scene.

I immediately started crying and explained to my mother what had happened and told her about the previous days when they were relentlessly bullying and taunting me. She compassionately listened to me, and yes, she went and talked to the bully's mother later that day. My mother always said, "There are three sides to a story. There is his side, her side, and the truth." She said that if you get all parties together, then you might be able to get the truth out of them. Even though I was mortified and angry about the fight, the situation did not turn out as bad as I thought.

I learned during that time that it was important for me to seek support from my family. This may help you do the same during your most difficult times. Life will sometimes beat you up physically, emotionally, spiritually, mentally, and even financially. Don't be afraid to reach out to friends, family, or a mental health professional for support. Talking about your struggles with a trusted family member or individual can help you gain perspective and find solutions.

The next day, the bully and her sisters came to apologize to me, prompted by their mother. Believe it or not, I no longer had any trouble with her or her friends. She even became a little friendlier towards me after that dreadful day. Someone told me that everyone thought I won the fight, and that's why she and her friends never bothered me again. I didn't care about winning that fight or any other. I didn't want to fight anyway. I was defending myself and decided not to offer any more of my cheeks.

That was the only physical fight I had as a child (My only violent incident). As I grew older and matured, I learned how to fight verbally with words, using my emotional intelligence instead of throwing punches. I was trained to use the correct de-escalation techniques that usually prevented potential violence. With these techniques, I learned how to prevent a situation from escalating to the point of verbal assault or physical battery.

After that horrible experience, I vowed as a child to never let anyone take my power away and make me feel small or helpless. I also vowed never to stand by and watch one person bully another without my protest. I didn't like the way my bully and her friends had made me feel, and I never wanted another human being to feel that way. Even at that age, I was a natural-born nurturer, but later, I developed the skills of a leader, protector, and healer.

Much later in life, I also vowed not to use my religious beliefs to judge and exclude another human being from receiving agape love and respect from me. I am not God, and I am not a judge. Judgment belongs to Him, the King of kings and the Conqueror of them all. Who am I to place judgment on anyone? I am only a vessel He uses to send a message of love, honor, and respect and bring glory to His Holy name.

My mother (much later) shared a story about when she was teased and bullied as a little girl, and how she overcame it. My mother was and still is one of the most incredible supporters in my life. I learned how to be a cheerleader for others by watching her cheer me on and cheer on other family members and friends in her life. She continued to share experiences from her own life to teach me lessons on several occasions when I was growing up.

I learned that overcoming adversity was a journey that required patience, resilience, and self-compassion by watching her example. She made us attend Bible class and church weekly. She not only talked the talk, but she walked the walk of a devout Christian woman. I also learned integrity, humility, and self-respect by watching her. I remember one of my mom's friends saying (to her), "Girl, you don't look like you've been through all that." She was right. My mom didn't look like the struggles she had been through.

Her beauty continued to shine inward and outward despite her struggles. She was one of the smartest and strongest women I knew. I wouldn't truly appreciate this fact until I went through my own struggles later as an adult. I drew inspiration from her stories of resilience and triumph over adversity. By overcoming her challenges, she gave me motivation to overcome mine.

Fast forward to about one and a half years after my first college graduation with an associate of science degree in fashion merchandising/marketing. At 19 ½, I wanted another challenge after becoming bored with my job at a fashion boutique in my hometown of Ft. Lauderdale. I wanted a new adventure and enlisted in the U.S. Air Force. Being away from home for many years frightened me, so I eased my way into the military as a reservist instead of active duty.

You see, I had lived a sheltered life and was still too afraid to venture out on my own, but this was a safe way to get wet by only dipping my toe in the water. I loved being a part of a team. I did not love being a leader. As a young adult, this was the first time anyone asked me to be a leader. Let me rephrase that: I was not asked; I was placed in the leadership role of dormitory chief, aka dorm chief.

The role of the dorm chief is to supervise the entire women's dorm during our time in basic training. She would be responsible for giving verbal commands to the ladies in the dorm and reporting back to the training instructor (T.I.) when someone misbehaved. In other words, being a snitch. I thought to myself, "Are you kidding me?" When I heard what my responsibilities would entail.

My T.I. (obviously) saw something (in me) that I did not see in myself. I was horrified and self-conscious at that time. I thought to myself,

"I am only nineteen years old. What do I know about being a leader?" My thoughts were running out of control even though I tried and tried; I did not feel comfortable in this new leadership role as the dorm chief!

I remember standing anxiously in front of the group, under the instruction of my T.I., to tell them to prepare for bed. I was nervous and trembling as I stood there. There were women in there much older than me that I thought would have been more qualified, yet I stood before them. I was about to place a verbal order for the first time. After completing that task, it was obvious to them (and me) that I lacked confidence in that role. It was not a comfortable place to be in. I felt mortified and defeated. Over the years, I learned to ignore my inner critic.

The next morning, during formation, I had to ensure that all the rows of women were lined up correctly and ready to march. The dorm chief had to have a big mouth to be heard by all the women in formation. My voice was almost like a quiet mouse at that time. I learned quickly to project my voice a little louder among the group. After about a week of this agony, I marched into my training instructor's office in the center of our dorm and gave up my position as dorm chief. "Airman Clayton reporting, ma'am." She gave me a mean, stern look and shouted, "What do you want, airmen?"

I gathered all my nerves to speak these words to her, "Airmen Clayton, reporting, I don't want to be dorm chief anymore." My heart was pounding hard in my chest, and my voice shook while I spoke those words to her. I expected to be verbally torn to shreds. Fortunately, she was not as harsh as she could have been, but she did yell a few words at me and told me to get out of her office. "Get out of my office, Airmen!" I looked humbly at her and replied as trained, "Ma'am, yes, ma'am."

I did an about-face movement and returned to my area of the dorm. The next morning, after we lined up in formation, our T.I. came and removed me from the dorm chief position in the lineup and placed me at the front of one of the squads. This was my first day as a squad leader, and I was only responsible for my squad. A squad is only the row of women that stood directly behind me in formation instead of the entire dorm. "Okay, this is not so bad." I thought to myself. Even though I was still in a leadership role, I was comfortable with this lesser position.

I realized that day, and several years ahead, that people saw me as a leader, even if I did not see it in myself yet. I started to embrace my leadership roles during my years in the Air Force Reserves, which followed me until I was honorably discharged and entered civilian life. I not only acquired and improved my leadership skills in the U.S. Air Force, but it was also where I fell in love for the first time.

We were both stationed at Shepard Air Force Base in Wichita Falls, Texas, and we lived in separate dorms for the men and women. The laundromat and the cafeteria were a few public places where we could co-mingle with the opposite sex. I remember our instructors telling us that no displays of affection (PDA) were allowed on base, so we could not kiss or hug each other in public. It was a structured and strict place, and I loved it! I was comfortable in this environment. After all, it reminded me of home.

We fell in love quickly, and I remember being together every day. As time progressed, we were inseparable and eventually married in the fall of that year. Our wedding day was beautiful. I remember thinking he was perfect, and our day was perfect, until we drove away into the sunset with his family, piled into a rented Lincoln Town car with us. Yes, that's right, you read that last sentence correctly. Instead of the bride and groom riding away into the sunset to start their new lives, his family joined us on our first ride together.

The fun fact about my wedding day is that we forgot to order our limousine for after the wedding, so we had no choice but to hitch a ride back to our hotel with his family. This was another lesson in adversity, where I learned that life is unpredictable and circumstances may change unexpectedly. I stayed flexible and open to adjusting my plans and expectations as needed on that day and primarily throughout my marriage.

Unfortunately, my fairytale marriage ended after nine years and two handsome sons later. I had to accept that I was a failure for the first time. I was disillusioned by my fairytale. We were both very young when we married, so we were doomed to fail because of our lack of relationship experience. He was my first love, but we did not know how to make it work without any great relationship examples.

In life, you should always have failure as an option because it will happen whether you want it to or not. It is inevitable. Although I had hoped my marriage would last a lifetime, it was not our destiny. You should be willing to fail just as often as you win, if not more. One of my mentors, Sir Dr. James Dentley, III, says about failure, "It's not an identity, it's an event." In other words, we should not wrap our identity up in failure but learn from it and move on.

It is only one event in your life, and it should not define you as a person. Don't take failure or success personally. Success comes after working hard. You only fail if you don't get back up and try again. If that doesn't work, then try something else. Look at it as a setback that you can learn from. View failure as an opportunity for growth. Analyze what went wrong, adjust your approach, and try again with newfound knowledge and resilience.

As a divorced mother of two, I would also gain inspiration from my friends' stories of resilience and triumph over adversity. Learning how others have overcome challenges can provide motivation and new perspectives in your own life. I then used my adversity as an opportunity for personal growth and self-discovery. I reflected on my values, strengths, and weaknesses and used this knowledge to navigate challenges more effectively in the future.

About two years after I became an R.N., I started to recognize good nurse leaders in various units in the civilian hospital where I worked. My knowledge grew as my experience improved. After a few months of developing my nursing skills in the (E.D.) emergency department, I was asked and convinced to train as a relief charge nurse and lead the night shift staff. Again, I did not feel ready to take on this enormous task in this 30+ beds E.D. My inner critic of doubt was rearing her ugly head again, and I had to silence her.

Yet again, I was being prepared to serve as a leader and reluctantly accepted the challenge. My leadership style as a charge nurse imitates the role of a servant-leader. When I am in the charge nurse role, I pride myself on being available for my nurses and our patients. I did not want to be like the lazy charge nurse who sits behind the desk most of the shift, barking orders at everyone. I wanted to be hands-on with the patients and even initiate their care as needed until seen by the physician.

I eventually began to like my role as charge nurse and took pride in being one of the best servant leaders during that time. Some charge nurses had a stern leadership style, almost like one of my T.I. drill sergeants in the military, and the staff would rebel against them. I preferred humility and wanted to assist my staff when necessary. I did not shout out orders and preferred simple discussions instead of negative verbal gymnastics with the team.

One of the nurses said (to me) when she arrived at work one night, "I am so happy when you are in charge because I know it will be a good shift!" Several team members would also say that to me, which always humbled me. It was confirmation that you can catch more bees with honey than with an iron fist.

Even today, when I am in the charge nurse role, if I notice one of my nurses having a rough shift, I will step in and assist them as needed. I will insist that the nurse take a few moments off the unit to regroup and get some fresh air while I care for their patients. I will never let my nurses go through a twelve-hour shift without taking a few moments to step away from their patient assignment.

It fills my heart with pride and joy to know that they like working as a part of my team and confirms that my leadership qualities promote a positive work environment in my unit. Building trust is always the goal. Once your staff trusts you as their fair, non-judgmental servant-leader, they will be more than willing to go the extra mile for you and your organization.

Believe it or not, I pray every chance for the staff and patients. I never tell them this, of course, because some of them may not believe in prayer or even believe in God. And you know what? That doesn't stop me from praying for them and praying for their well-being, especially the ones who are in pain and dying.

I immediately started working on ways to take away their pain. I sometimes use distractions like offering an ice pack, the television in the room, a warm blanket, or having a pleasant conversation with them until the doctor arrives. Several times, I've had patients tell me they feel better after being heard and having someone care about their concerns.

Sometimes, their pain is not only physical, but some have more mental anguish and a few stated feelings of spiritual emptiness at times. "I guess I just needed somebody to listen to me." One patient would tell me. You'd be surprised how many people are lonely and don't have anyone to talk to and/or care about their well-being. It is sad for some people, so I often offer compassion with a listening ear.

If you have someone who (really) cares about you, whether they're annoying or not, you must count your blessings. Some people wish they had that type of annoying attention, caring, and love from someone.

During my journey, I also had to learn how to practice self-care. I not only care for my physical side but also attend to my spiritual, emotional, financial, and mental well-being. I recharged my batteries by engaging in activities that enhanced my joy and relaxation, such as Pilates, yoga, meditation, or spending time with my loved ones. Remember that self-care is not selfish, and it is okay to put yourself first sometimes.

You will come back to your family with a renewed mind and spirit. You will have a more positive outlook while feeling more motivated to press on. Wait for that breakthrough. Your breakthrough is coming. Remember, overcoming adversity is a journey that requires patience, resilience, and self-compassion. By implementing these suggestions and staying committed to your well-being, you can rise above adversity and emerge stronger on the other side.

I created this little poem after a stressful night when one of my patients was close to dying of a heart attack. Thankfully, after we resuscitated him, he pulled through and completely recovered after spending about two weeks in the hospital.

An ER Nurse's Prayer by Sabrina Clayton©

In the rush of the emergency room's night, the nurse prays for her patient with all her might.
With silent whispers to the heavens above, she's seeking solace and seeking love.
As the patient's breath grows faint and thin, she prays for a miracle to begin.
With faith that shines through the darkest night, she holds onto hope, so pure and bright.
And in a moment that defies all fears, the patient stirs, and hope appears!
A gasp, a heartbeat, a miraculous turn,
The nurse keeps praying for their heart that burns.
Her patient is in the dance of life and death's embrace,
A bond is formed in a moment of grace.
In the echo of prayers, hope is found,
As her patient's heart beats again, a beautiful sound!

I don't know what your beliefs are. I believe it will not be difficult for God to help you through your situation in your life. It will not take any effort for Him to lift you out of your darkness. Please remain humble and grateful in your time of suffering. I know that sounds difficult, maybe even impossible, but you must trust and believe. I believe God is worthy of praise at the beginning, middle, and end of your trials. Sometimes, He may even humble us down before He blesses us again.

What is your belief? Do you have something or someone to believe in? A Higher Power? Then, please tap into that belief system and go after your dreams. Think of your challenges as obstacles you must overcome through hard work, and you will not be defeated! Don't be afraid of hard work. You are more than a conqueror through Him that loved you, according to Romans 8:37 in the Bible. Whether you are religious or just spiritual, whatever your belief system is, hold onto it and use it to strengthen you in times of difficulty.

This brings my story to the present day (today) while I am living my best life. This is the future that I dreamed of in the past. I have worked hard, with God's help, and enjoy nicer blessings today because of that. I also practice self-care through a healthier diet, exercise, reading, writing, keeping a (personal) journal, and taking time off for extra rest and relaxation. All these activities help promote self-discovery and improvement in all areas of my life. I treasure my friendships: old friends and even a few new ones.

My life is full of joy, peace, grace, and love. My cup runneth over. All these experiences taught me how to be more resilient and not let my struggles defeat me. With my belief in God as my guide and protector, I was destined to succeed in any path I chose if I gave Him glory with each step.

My idea of success and your idea of success may be completely different. What is your idea of success? How do you rise above diversity in your life? Do you take your lemons and make a decadent dessert like lemon cakes, cookies, or lemon bars? Do you prefer lemonade? What about squeezing those lemons over a nice piece of lobster tail or fresh shrimp? Use your imagination and get creative with rising above your adversity.

I want to encourage everyone going through their (own) personal trials to hold on! You can get through it. Some of us have heard the saying, "If He brings you to it, He will bring you through it!" One of my favorite verses in the Bible is Philippians 4:13, which reads, "I can do all things through Christ who strengthens me." I can and I will. You can and you will.

I am stronger and wiser today because of my earlier struggles and challenges in my young life. Both my sons are grown and thriving citizens within their communities. They learned how to be resilient through their (own) challenges in life from witnessing how I handled my own. Are their lives perfect? No, not at all, and neither is mine. But I believe they have everything they need to survive, even after I am long gone.

As parents, we know that most of our children will do what we do and not do as we say. If you suffer from anxiety, then you may raise anxious children. If you suffer from depression, then your children may absorb those negative emotions as well. We need to focus on the positive aspects of our lives and practice gratitude for the things we have. This mindset shift can help us maintain our perspective during tough times. Remember, you don't look like what you've been through, and you are still here, Persevering, Believing, Healing, Loving, and Forgiving. If you allow yourself to maintain your faith and strength while going through your trials and tribulations? Eventually, you will be led to transformation, empowerment, and success!

Give yourself goals to achieve and live up to your expectations. Keep your head up. Keep your spirit up. Keep your eyes on the prize. You must start believing you can do whatever you set your mind to do! Then you must do the work! Remember, life is not perfect, but you will fail if you don't try. You lose if you don't stand up after falling down. You lose if you stop after you fail. You only lose if you stop. If you don't try again, you will fail by default. If you have life, then you have a chance. Take that chance! If you allow yourself to maintain your faith and strength while going through your trials and tribulations, eventually, you will be led to a road of transformation, empowerment, and success!

Keep your imagination alive and dream big! I dare you to dream while you journey through this life because there is no expiration date on your dreams! As long as you keep rising out of bed in the morning, you have another chance to win. You may fail again and again, but don't stop. Keep rising! That's right, rise everyone! Rise up to your feet! Rise up to your potential! Rise up to your dreams! Your goals! You can rise above adversity and become what you were meant to be! You are more than a conqueror, and you have already won – now Rise up and let's get to work. You got this!

About The Author

Sabrina Clayton

Sabrina Clayton is a registered nurse with over 14 years of experience working in the emergency department with an extensive nursing background. She began nursing training and career at the Community College of the Air Force in the 1990s. She graduated as a medical service specialist and later advanced her training to be a licensed practical (vocational) nurse. She went back to school to major in business and nursing. She received a Bachelor of Science degree in nursing from Florida Atlantic University and a Bachelor of Science degree in business from Nova Southeastern University.

Sabrina has also worked in Corporate America for eight years and learned how to navigate through her financial challenges. During those corporate years, Sabrina learned important investment strategies that helped her purchase her first home in South Florida. She was a divorced mother with two young sons who eagerly learned how to buy and sell stocks. After her portfolio grew, she started investing more in real estate and purchasing land lots across America. She continues learning and expanding her mind, exploring new horizons, and being open to change.

Sabrina has developed strategies to systematically overcome any physical, emotional, spiritual, mental, or financial challenge that may arise. These strategies will assist the person with developing strength in any of these areas and becoming more resilient over time. However, they must put in the work! They will also learn to silence their inner critic and move beyond the self-defeating words of doubt, fear, and insecurity.

Sabrina's vision is clear: to be a cheerleader for humanity. Her goal is to share with the readers how she overcame and is still overcoming some adversities in her life. Her life is not perfect, but she knows how to adapt to any situation through her faith and support from family and friends. She has acquired many skills that she has shared with clients, friends, and family. She always uses problems and adversity to propel her to the next level.

On June 23, 2020, during the height of the COVID-19 pandemic, Sabrina was a guest on The Hangin With Web Show, where she was interviewed by the host and journalist GW Pomichter. She was also interviewed on May 14, 2020, by Sonia Allen on The Notable Ones podcast and on May 1, 2020, by Chris Baker on the Friday Night Author Roundtable radio show, to name a few.

Sabrina is also the author of two children's books, My Cartoon Imagination at School, and My Cartoon Imagination at the Hospital. She invites you to take this fun-filled journey with her main character, Samara, as she explores her vivid imagination in these creative and poetic stories. Both books are educational, using sight words sprinkled throughout with a little inspirational message at the end of each book. They both contain moments of bravery, understanding, and optimism. These traits help children become more open to receiving the care they need at medical institutions and while interacting at school.

She hopes her books will inspire children to never give up on their dreams, even if there are roadblocks and setbacks along the way. The children can tap into their imaginary superpowers and visualize themselves victorious in any situation.

12

Unmasking Authenticity A Self-Discovering Journey

Melissa Farmer-Hill

The phrase, "Just be yourself," is so common, but how often do we truly embody it? In today's world, we're bombarded with images of seemingly perfect lives on social media, making us question why we don't measure up. Whether it's seeing friends with their new cars or colleagues getting promotions, we often find ourselves asking, "Why can't this be me?" Instead of confronting this question head-on, we often resort to wearing masks, hiding our true selves, pretending everything is fine. We bury our feelings deep inside, unaware that this self-denial is a form of emotional abuse.

Living behind these masks prevents us from being authentic, trapping us in an emotional prison of our own making. This can lead to a host of issues, including low self-esteem, constant people-pleasing, and a sense of isolation, as we believe no one can really understand our true selves. As we strive to maintain this facade, our lives become increasingly stressful and exhausting, devoid of the sustainability that comes with living authentically.

Now is the time to break free from these illusions. Instead of expending energy on upholding an image that doesn't align with our true selves, it's time to embrace authenticity. If you're someone who's always seeking personal growth and striving to be the best version of yourself, continue reading as we embark on a journey of self-discovery and acceptance.

What masks do you wear? We all wear different masks, concealing various parts of ourselves from the world. I vividly recall the first time I realized I was hiding behind a mask; mine was the mask of people-pleasing. It was during a weekend visit to my dad's house. It was his weekend to have me over, but my cousin on my mom's side was having a birthday party, so he had to drop me off and pick me up. My dad, a Jehovah's Witness who does not celebrate birthdays, was displeased that I was going, but despite having a great time when he picked me up, I told him that the party was just "okay." I mentioned that I did not participate in singing "Happy Birthday."

Even at age nine, I understood the situation but chose to lie to seek my dad's approval. To my surprise, he and my stepmom were proud that I had resisted the temptation to join in singing. This experience planted a seed in me, equating attention, happiness, and fulfillment with doing things that pleased others, even if it meant sacrificing my desires. This belief became deeply ingrained in me, leading me to believe that seeking approval through conformity was the path to acceptance and love. This pattern of behavior persisted for decades, shaping my interactions and decisions.

Although I was too young to grasp it fully, my tendency to prioritize others' approval over my well-being gradually chipped away at my self-esteem. I found myself unhappy when I couldn't meet someone else's expectations of me. Two specific instances from my youth come to mind where I felt inadequate but lacked the tools to address those feelings. Have you ever experienced such emotions? Even as an adult, where you struggled to confront and deal with a specific person or situation that led you to internalize it negatively?

I can recall an incident from my childhood when I eagerly ran home from school to proudly show my family a B grade on a paper I worked hard to earn. I was beaming with pride as I told my uncle and his girlfriend about my grade. However, my excitement quickly turned to disappointment when my uncle said, "Why didn't you get an A?" His words hit me like a ton of bricks. I felt a wave of inadequacy wash over me, as if all my efforts were insufficient to meet his expectations. From that moment on, I decided never to show anyone my grades unless they were A's, convinced that anything less meant I was stupid. I stopped seeking help, even when I struggled, and became adept at hiding my true emotions. As an adult, how often have you allowed others' opinions to shape your self-perception, causing you to doubt your abilities and self-worth?

Another memory that shaped my self-image occurred in elementary school with my teacher, who we'll call Mr. S. During one class session, Mr. S. asked us who we aspired to be when we grew up. When my turn came, I enthusiastically said that I wanted to be like Nadia Comaneci, an Olympic gymnast who won the gold medal and scored a perfect 10, almost unheard of at that time. I believed I could achieve this dream because of my cheerleading skills; I could do several flips, back-bends, and splits. Plus, I was already on the pep squad, not old enough to be a cheerleader yet. However, Mr. S. told me I was too tall and long to be a gymnast and then compared me to one of my classmates, saying they would love someone like T. I will call her T for the sake of this writing. His words cut deep, and that night, I found myself praying and crying, questioning why God made me so tall and asking if he could make me short.

I carried Mr. S.'s words with me until eighth grade. It was then that my teacher, whom we'll call Ms. N., reassured me that I was more than the opinions of others. This affirmation came at a critical time when I believed I wasn't good enough to perform a solo for graduation. Ms. N.'s encouragement stayed with me through high school, where I eventually graduated with honors. These experiences taught me firsthand how damaging it can be when someone belittles your body image, especially at a young age.

Can you recall any experiences from your past where someone's words or actions belittled you, leaving a lasting impact on your self-esteem and emotional well-being? Do you still allow others to define who you are or who you should be? Conversely, can you remember those who affirmed you, giving you the confidence to move beyond your doubts and perceptions of yourself?

After high school, I drifted through various jobs without a clear plan. I suppose it was because I lacked the knowledge or drive to attend college, even though I did take a few classes. However, there was never any real commitment on my part. By this time, I had met someone and made him the priority in my life, hoping he would fill the void I felt. Have you ever put your needs on the back burner for the sake of a relationship? If so, you understand what I was going through. My life revolved around our activities after work and on the weekends. As long as I had a job, I was content.

While I thought having a college degree was nice, I was ignorant of the fact that in the 90s, a college degree was critical for opening doors to the future. This realization hit me when I got a position as a clerk in the fundraising department of the Little City Foundation in Palatine, Illinois. I loved it. I wanted to move up within the company. However, I soon realized that my lack of a formal education, (specifically) a college degree, hindered any possibility of advancement.

I knew that if I didn't do something, I would be stuck handling paperwork, ensuring signatures and forms were filled out correctly, instead of coordinating and making fundraising deals, like bringing in Chicago Bears and Bulls players to fundraise for the Foundation. This was the first time in years that I felt like I didn't measure up. I felt like I was stupid all over again. I was in a relationship without any hope for progress and still living at home.

I began to question myself and my life choices. Should I have taken out a loan for school? Were the people in higher positions better than me? I beat myself up, but this time, it wasn't triggered by someone else's words; it was self-inflicted. This time, I failed me. Despite being in a place full of opportunities, I didn't have the qualifications to seize them. Suddenly, what felt like a regular life was really "the struggle." I didn't realize I was struggling until I saw what a better opportunity looked like.

The saying "When preparation meets opportunity" struck a chord within me, revealing a sense of unpreparedness waiting quietly and desperately beneath the surface. I believed that obtaining a degree would give me a sense of importance and boost my self-esteem significantly. I saw it as a clear-cut solution—I needed that degree to become somebody. The only option I knew could help me pay for college was joining the Army. Without hesitation, I was determined that a degree would transform my identity, making me feel important.

At the time, as far as I knew, no one in my family had a college degree. So, imagine their surprise when I returned from the recruiting office and announced to my family and my boyfriend, I enlisted in the Army full-time and would be leaving within the month. It put them in a state of shock. It was a bold move, but I was ready to break away from my fear and pursue something I believed would make me extraordinary regardless of who and what I had to let go. This decision marked a turning point in my life. I embarked on a journey that would shape my future and challenge me in ways I had never imagined.

For every moment I doubted myself, the Army provided me with a platform for transformation. It taught me to project confidence, command authority, communicate effectively, and take ownership of my responsibilities. The military instilled in me the ability to remain calm and composed under immense pressure, shaping me into a resilient and capable individual, regardless of my educational background. Despite not having a college degree initially, I was driven to pursue further education. Within my first two years, I earned my associate's degree, followed by my bachelor's degree a few years later. I was determined to pave my path to a successful career. I was selected as a Warrant Officer Human Resources Technician four years later.

Being a Warrant Officer meant being a technical expert in my field within the Army. The Army was no easy journey, and I faced my fair share of challenges. Still, every ounce of effort I put in was returned to me tenfold, resulting in a rewarding military career that I am immensely proud of. I was privileged to serve alongside some of the most exceptional and dedicated individuals you will ever meet.

My commitment and contributions were recognized with prestigious awards such as The Douglas MacArthur Leadership Award (Germany), the Army Recruiting Ring, and the Army Human Resources Warrant Officer Instructor of the Year Award. I had the honor of working directly for the Secretary of the Army at the Pentagon and received over 20 military awards and decorations. I even graced the cover of the Army Recruiter Magazine. However, the badge I cherish the most is my Air Assault badge. I earned it during my service with the renowned 101st Airborne Division in Fort Campbell, Kentucky. I earned this badge learning how to rappel from helicopters. A skill I proudly showcase before almost every keynote speech I deliver by yelling, AIR ASSAULT!

Reflecting on my journey, I am grateful for the opportunities and experiences that shaped me. Serving in the Army was not just a job, but a calling I wholeheartedly embraced. It's a profession that continues to enrich my life even after retirement, and it is truly a gift that keeps on giving. After twenty fulfilling years, I retired from the Army with a heart full of gratitude and ready to embark on my next chapter.

Committing yourself to a greater cause is an immensely fulfilling experience. It allows you to discover a sense of purpose and contentment that transcends any other personal achievement. What experiences have you had that have brought you a similar sense of fulfillment and contentment?

As I prepared to leave the Army, I believed I was equipped to handle the transition to civilian life. However, I quickly discovered that the emotional toll was more profound than anticipated. Leaving behind the structured environment of the military, where I felt a clear sense of belonging and purpose, left me adrift and invisible in the civilian world. I felt important in the Army, but now, I felt like just another face in the crowd among the eight billion people walking the earth daily.

My initial excitement and anticipation for this new chapter soon gave way to anxiety and, eventually, depression. I found myself withdrawing from the world, only going through the motions of daily tasks like appointments and grocery shopping. I gathered solace in familiar comforts like spending time with my family and a few friends occasionally. Still, these fleeting moments of excitement couldn't fill the deep void I felt inside.

Instead, I spent hours on social media, binge-watching movies, overindulging in comfort foods, and consuming more wine than I should have. Coupled with my lack of sleep, averaging only 3-4 hours a night. Each day felt like a painful cycle of exhaustion and emptiness.

It was a family member who recognized the signs of depression in me and gently suggested that I seek help. At first, I was in denial; seeking help seemed like a sign of weakness, something I, as a strong, resilient woman, should not need. However, I came to realize that many women who have served in the military carry invisible scars that can profoundly impact their mental, emotional, and physical well-being long after their service has ended.

Often overlooked or misunderstood, these scars can manifest in various ways, hindering their ability to lead fulfilling lives after service. As a Black woman, the idea of therapy clashed with my cultural upbringing; my community often emphasizes resilience through prayer and talking it over with family. However, as I saw my situation deteriorating, I knew a change was necessary because this was not the life I had envisioned for my retirement.

Have you ever found yourself in a situation where seeking help went against your cultural or personal beliefs? How did you navigate this internal conflict, and what did you learn from the experience?

I was in therapy for nearly a year. I saw myself as an ideal patient because I was committed to getting better. The therapy proved invaluable in helping me process, manage, and address my mental health challenges, equipping me with the resilience I needed to navigate through my depression.

Reflecting on my healing journey, I realized my self-worth had long been tied to my military career. I sought validation through my achievements, believing that my rank, awards, and assignments measured my worth. However, transitioning into civilian life prompted a shift in this belief. I began to understand that true self-acceptance comes from within, independent of external validation. I no longer needed to seek approval through my accomplishments because I recognized my inherent value beyond my military career.

This realization brought me liberation and challenges. It was liberating because I no longer felt pressured to prove myself to others constantly. It was challenging because it meant confronting neglected parts of myself while chasing external acceptance. I had to face my fears, insecurities, doubts head-on, and beliefs about myself, which was daunting.

Through this process, I began to uncover my true self—the person beyond the uniform and accolades. I discovered that my self-worth was not contingent on my achievements or others' opinions but on my intrinsic value as a human being. Embracing my flaws and imperfections, I realized they are an integral part of who I am.

Letting go of the need for external validation allowed me to focus on what truly mattered to me. I pursued my passions and interests not to impress others but because they brought me joy and fulfillment. Rediscovering my creativity and reigniting my love for writing, speaking, and supporting others brought a renewed sense of purpose.

This journey of self-discovery taught me that true happiness comes from self-acceptance and self-love. It's about embracing yourself for who you are, not who others want you to be. While my military career will always be a large part of my existence, it no longer defines me. I am more than my achievements or past; I am me, which is enough.

Have you ever experienced a shift in how you perceive your self-worth? What prompted this change, and how did it impact your life?

World-famous author, speaker, and coach Tony Robbins often emphasizes the two main forces that drive human behavior. #1) the desire to avoid pain and #2) the desire to gain pleasure. This concept suggests that much of our actions and decisions are motivated by seeking pleasure or avoiding pain.

Reflecting on my own life, I realized I joined the Army to escape the pain of feeling inadequate. However, after twenty years of service, I faced similar feelings upon returning home. Inadequacy can be a powerful and overwhelming emotion, leaving us with a sense of not measuring up or being unworthy. These feelings often arise from comparing ourselves to others and setting unrealistic expectations. Or from past experiences that have shaped our self-perception.

My journey taught me ten valuable lessons that helped me overcome these feelings. I would like to share them with you, along with reflection questions to help you gain insight into your own experiences:

1. **Practice Self-Compassion**: Stop beating yourself up if it's not perfect. Treat yourself with the same kindness and understanding you would offer a friend facing similar feelings. Acknowledge that it's normal to have doubts and imperfections, but keep moving forward. How do you typically respond to your own imperfections or moments when things aren't perfect? What steps can you take to treat yourself with more kindness and understanding in those situations?

2. **Challenge Negative Thoughts**: Did you know that we can have up to 60,000 thoughts per day, and up to 70% are negative? When you catch yourself thinking negatively about yourself or your

situation, challenge those thoughts, learn to sit with them, and see where they are coming from. Ask yourself if there's evidence to support these thoughts or if you're just being too hard on yourself. How do you think you could become more aware of your negative thoughts and challenge them when they arise? What strategies might help you shift toward more positive and constructive thinking patterns?

3. **Dream Big and Set Realistic Goals:** Striking a balance is important. Dreaming big encourages growth beyond what you think you can achieve. By breaking down your goals into manageable steps and celebrating those small victories (along the way) that keep you moving forward, you will be amazed at how easily you can turn those dreams into reality. What's your approach to goal setting and balancing big dreams with practical steps? What small victories have you celebrated recently helped you progress toward your larger goals?

4. **Focus on Your Strengths and Acknowledge Your Weaknesses:** You are who you are. However, focusing on your strengths while acknowledging your weaknesses can be powerful for personal growth. Embracing this mindset allows you to leverage your strengths to achieve your goals while addressing areas for improvement, which can be worked on at any time you decide. How do you currently identify and leverage your strengths to pursue your goals? How do you approach addressing areas for improvement without feeling discouraged?

5. **Seek Support:** Talk to a trusted friend or family member, and network with positive people who only want to see you WIN! Do you have a support system of friends, family, or mentors who encourage and uplift you? How can you connect with more positive people who will support your journey?

6. **Practice Mindfulness:** Remaining present and attentive to the current situation is crucial. Avoid dwelling on the past because it can leave you feeling like a victim. Remember, your future outlook is a direct reflection of your present actions. Practicing mindfulness can help you release those self-critical thoughts and alleviate anxieties about what lies ahead. How do you practice mindfulness daily to stay focused on the present moment? What techniques have you found most helpful in letting go of self-critical thoughts and reducing anxiety about the future?

7. **Engage in Self-Care:** Self-care extends beyond our wonderful spa days, although it can and should be a component. It involves meeting your emotional, physical, occupational, intellectual, financial, social, environmental, and spiritual needs. Engaging in activities that nourish these aspects of your life can boost your well-being and self-esteem. How do you currently prioritize these different aspects of self-care in your life? Are there any areas you feel you could pay more attention to?

8. **Learn from Mistakes:** In a world where admitting mistakes can be challenging, have you considered that acknowledging them could be the first step toward valuable growth and learning? Rather than seeing mistakes as failures, they can be viewed as opportunities for personal development. What insights have you gained from reflecting on your past mistakes?

9. **Set Boundaries:** This is a big one for most, whether establishing healthy boundaries in your relationships and activities. Learn to say no to things that drain or make you feel inadequate. How do you currently navigate setting boundaries in your relationships and activities? Are there areas where you struggle to say no, even when it's necessary for your well-being?

10. **Seek Professional Help:** If feelings of inadequacy persist and interfere with your daily life, consider seeking help from a mental health professional. Therapy can provide strategies to overcome these feelings and improve self-esteem.

Even after implementing these practices, my journey was far from over. Following therapy, I felt ready to tackle life head-on. I recognized a significant gap in the transition from military to civilian life, so I took it upon myself to bridge that gap. I began by volunteering at my local Veterans of Foreign Wars (VFW) as part of the Veteran Service Officer team, helping my fellow Veterans navigate the military benefit process. This experience showed me that many women faced similar challenges during this transition. They battled depression, anxiety, and a sense of uncertainty about their next life chapter.

After conducting further research, I uncovered a startling fact: women often experience more emotional distress than men when separating from the military. This realization inspired me to create the SHERO COFFEE CLUB. A social enterprise committed to keeping the world caffeinated and women celebrated. I envisioned it as a unique platform to honor and amplify the stories of women who have served. Each bag of coffee features a woman military Veteran and a brief narrative about her service, ensuring that her sacrifice and achievements are recognized and remembered.

But my efforts didn't stop at coffee. I expanded the company to offer SHERO communication, self-care, and vision board workshops tailored for Veteran women. Additionally, we launched the SHERO Gallery on our website, showcasing videos of Veterans sharing their stories and how they overcame challenges. My goal is simple: it is all worthwhile if these efforts can support even one woman in becoming the best version of herself or help her take the first step.

Shifting my perspective on life was crucial; I realized that taking full responsibility for my mindset was key to thriving in all aspects of self-care. Seeking the necessary help was a game-changer, and now, I'm dedicated to making each day great by envisioning the life I desire and putting in the work to manifest it. I've adopted a "Be, Do, and Have" mentality: first, I embody the qualities I admire (be), which leads to actions (do) that allow me to achieve my goals (have). How do you envision your ideal life, and what steps are you taking to make that vision a reality?

I pray that life continues to be a beautiful journey of self-discovery for you, my friend. May you thrive at each stage in the process. As always, be brilliant, be you, be blessed!

About The Author

Melissa Farmer-Hill

Melissa Farmer-Hill is a retired Army Veteran, Author, Workshop Leader, and Entrepreneur. She holds a Master's in Event and Tourism Management from Roosevelt University.

Melissa Farmer-Hill has served worldwide as an Army Human Resources Warrant Officer with deployments to Iraq and Kosovo. Melissa has been recognized throughout her service with prestigious awards such as The Douglas MacArthur Leadership Award, the Army Recruiting Ring, and the Army Human Resources Instructor of the Year. Additionally, she has received over 20 other military awards and decorations. Recently, Melissa was selected as a recipient of Empower to Enlightens' 2024 I AM EVERY WOMAN Award.

Her book "Army Strong Women" tells the untold stories of countless women who have served in the military. The book explores the challenges, prejudices, and opportunities these women encountered while pursuing a career in the Army.

Melissa Farmer-Hill is the CEO of SHERO Coffee Club, LLC, a social enterprise coffee brand dedicated to honoring the service, sacrifice, and achievements of women who have served. Her mission is to keep the world caffeinated and women motivated. Melissa hosts workshops year-round where veteran women can come together to create, dream, grow, and connect. She is also the curator of SHERO UNCORKED, an annual celebration providing a platform for women veterans to share their journeys and experiences from the stage. Additionally, Melissa is the co-owner of Farmer & Hill Enterprise alongside her husband. They specialize in short-term rentals and real estate.

Melissa serves as a member of the Veterans Services Officer Team for VFW Post 311 in Richton Park, Illinois, with a special focus on building positive relationships with women Veterans seeking military benefits.

She is a lifetime member of the Benjamin O. Davis Post 311. A National Women Veterans United (NWVU) member and the Verna L. Jones, American Legion Post #478. Melissa has an unwavering commitment to service and community far beyond her years of military service.

13

How He Kept Me
Verlin White

As a little girl, I always dreamed of being a superstar with a small round object in my hand called a pearl, and I didn't know what that meant. I got teased and made fun of because of my nose, big eyes, and thumb in my mouth. I thought that was impossible. I never liked to take pictures. I would tear them up behind people's backs so I would not be exploited because I did not like seeing myself.

One day, Mrs. Becky started singing a song: My Bonnie lies over the ocean, my Bonnie lies over the sea, oh bring her back, bring her back, oh God bring her back to me, to me, oh bring back my Bonnie to me. I asked her to sing it over and over. Then I asked her why God brought her back. Mrs. Becky said Bonnie was very special to God. Bonnie was afraid she did not know God would protect her, so God kept calling her back. I told Mrs. Becky I wanted to be Bonnie, and from that day forward, I asked people to call me Bonnie.

I was four years old. I felt empowered because someone went to the depths of the sea to come and get me. I had a problem. I felt so ugly and horrible that no one would like me or the way I looked. I enjoyed watching the little rascals because I could relate to Buckwheat. In my mind, this was me, and I liked to follow and watch everything and would tattle-tell on everyone. Well, that did not make me popular, but others knew not to act up around me. Five years later, my facial features changed, which was a bad experience in my mind. I cried out to God and asked why he made me so ugly.

I wanted to be the beautiful girl (Bonnie) you brought from over the sea because you loved me. Make me beautiful, at least pleasing to the eye. This was the first time I heard a voice saying not long, your eyes will be open, and you will see what I see.

A year went by, and I started to feel different on the inside. I do not know how to explain it. My hair grew, I started dressing better, and people would say I looked different. I was so excited about the transformation. Then, a shift happened, and I began to hear the cries of others with no face, and I would feel their pain. One day, outside of my bedroom, one of those voices came from my mother's room, and all I could do was cry. I felt her loneliness. My mother was alone in her room because my father left her to see another woman. I wanted to go into her room, comfort her, and sleep with her, but I was too big for that and did not want her to know I heard her crying.

Every night before bed, I sat between the bedrooms. One night, my father asked me to go to bed. I said not until I knew my mother was okay. He said she was asleep. Little did he know I could feel her tender heart and could not tell him because he was the source of her pain. I called out and asked God what I should do. He said to see Mrs. Becky, so I did. She taught me how to pray, and release things to God; He would show me what to do in due time. Well, what does that mean? I asked. This went on for months. One Sunday, I went to church, and my mother said I had to watch after my younger sister and not let her out of my sight. So, I took her to church, gave my life to God, and told my younger sister, since mom said I must watch you, you are coming with me. I made her give her life to God! That was not a bad thing. We were baptized that night, and my life was never the same.

The friends I had, I no longer wanted to be around them. This was a defining moment for me. Little did I know that those same friends made different life decisions. One went into prostitution and had a baby, and the other became a drug addict. I often wondered which one I would have been if I didn't give my life to God. A couple of years later, the family I used to hang around was in a car accident, speeding. Because we were that close, I would have been in the car. Multiple people died. My friend's baby died, her mother, brother, and sister's baby died. I was devastated. All I could say was that I was supposed to be with them that day, but God did not allow me to.

Remember, God told me I was not going to be living in Michigan, and shortly after my aunt died, my journey began. Little did I know that my big sister was devastated because they did not know where I was. I packed my bag and left for Chicago. I had a lot of family there, so they notified my parents that I was there.

I met an older woman who had diabetes, and she loved God so much that I was instantly drawn to her. Her family seemed to ignore her and her health issues. She taught me how to give her insulin injections. I sat at her feet and learned that her walk with God was so special, and no one knew who she (really) was. In my eyes, only famous people, like Pastors and other leaders, had such a relationship with God. The months ahead that I spent with her were priceless. I felt she would only be here on earth for a bit longer. Then, she went home to be with the Lord. I lost my first true Godly friend. Where would I find someone to spend time with and learn about this God? The God I was passionate about!

Later, I had the pleasure of babysitting a precious jewel. I went to get the baby a change of clothes when I heard a gunshot. I tipped toed out of the room to get to the baby. To my surprise, the man did not see me. However, I saw him. I grabbed the baby and held her tight so she would not say anything. I knew if he heard any noise, it would be over because the shooter was not aware of anyone else in the apartment. It was by the grace of God the baby made no noise. I hid under the bed and covered it in case the shooter decided to look around to make sure no one was there. When the coast was clear, I ran out fast with the baby and called my cousin and asked her to call an ambulance for the man who was shot. My cousin came and got me to make sure I was okay. An hour later, the word on the street was that the shooter had been caught. This was the second death I have avoided. Witnessing a murder in the hood will get you killed.

My next journey was to Louisiana. I call Louisiana 'The mother homeland' because that's where my parents grew up. I am not an adult yet. I left at age sixteen, and my peers graduated at eighteen and nineteen. Here, I met a lady who could not read, but she could read the bible. Once again, I was drawn to her. I stayed at her feet, learning everything I could about God and relationships. I was so fascinated with her passion for God and reading this book as a great educator would and not an illiterate person. I later found out from reading the word of God that she loved reading it so much that she became a teacher. She lived alone.

Across the street was a handsome young man living with his grandmother. She noticed he was looking at me. When he left, I felt drawn to visit with the grandmother, and once again, I was blown away by the quality of great women who love God unconditionally. It was strange that no one knew, but I did. She said she wanted someone to come and read the bible to her someday. It was my great pleasure to read every day I was there. She asked me to go to the store for her, and her grandson took me. He said, "I don't know what you did, but she loves you and never lets anyone in the house." I told him I love to see people who genuinely love God, and she is amazing. I spent a year in Louisiana with two outstanding women. I wanted to stay longer, but I had to go. My assignment from God was over in this city.

My next journey was to Texas. After arriving in the Lone Star State, I was notified months later that both my friends in Louisiana had died. They had the kindest things to say as if their life was whole because of me. It gives me tears to know I have helped someone fulfill their life. The atmosphere in Texas was different than the former places I had visited.

This time, I encountered my aunt, who loved God and would preach salvation to get you saved no matter what. I have not witnessed this level yet. I was perplexed by this, and she explained things to me. Many needed the devil cast out of them. However, I was still young and learning the ins and outs of my calling.

I later met an angry woman who could care less about her creator. Well, this is getting interesting! To my surprise, it was not the journey I was expecting. She thought I was a joke, and how can anyone so young think they love God? She said, "You are not even an adult; you are still wet behind the ears." Surprisingly enough, I was not afraid of this type of spirit. I started questioning the dark side and how to give love when there is so much sorrow. I was in a fight and did not know it. A fight called spiritual warfare. My aunt was a warrior. She taught me how to understand that I had the authority to allow demons to tremble in my presence, and fear was not an option.

I went back into the fiery pit and became close to this woman, and she threw all manner of evil towards me, and I countered it with love. She asked if she could talk to me, and I said of course. She said no one cared for me like you, and you were unafraid. Are you an angel? I smiled and hugged this 600lb+ woman. She smelled so bad that I had to ask if I could bathe her. She wondered how a 201-pound woman was going to handle her. We laughed, and I said one inch at a time. After being around some powerful women reading the Word of God to me, the challenges they rose from began to rise in me. All this LOVE must now conquer sin. Suddenly, the scriptures came alive, and I began to identify, in observance, the many types of personalities. I met a man who operated in the prophetic and deliverance. I was drawn to him to learn what God needed me to understand. Then, I was on my way to the next assignment.

My next journey was to California. All I heard was study, hear, listen, and do. I had no idea what to expect from this place. This atmosphere seemed more severe. Like I was about to experience a fear I could never have imagined. So, I was in a place to trust no one.

I met my sisters from my father's side for the first time, and they had a passion for God. I was excited to know this because I wanted some family to connect with. I spent some time with them; they were close to my age. I was excited to babysit my nephew while my sisters attended choir rehearsal. A man came to the door and said he was my sister's Pastor, so I welcomed him inside. I love God and the word, so we should get along just fine. He started acting strange and began to walk towards me. I told him that the Blood of Jesus covers me, and he said I will also. His actions were not funny or cute. He started reaching for my clothes, and I told God forgive me, but I am going to hit this man of God. He grabbed my blouse, ripped it off, and pulled his pants off. I screamed, and my nephew screamed, and this man threw twenty dollars at me and fled the house. What was this money for? I thought, was it hush money or for the inconvenience? I was confused. Either way, I did not want it. I felt awful and wondered if I did anything to bring this on. Suddenly, I felt God's heart grieve and say, there were many like this.

I went to grab my nephew and gave him a big hug; he saved my life from a rape in my sister's house. The next day, I called the church to report it, and a young elder came out and tried to do the same thing. My nephew rescued me again. I left my sister's house because I no longer felt safe. I needed more training, so I went to Southern California, where I met my first Pastor, Fred Price. I stayed there for years to study, hear, listen, and do. I finally went to college and pursued a nursing career. At least, this is what I thought I wanted. My story continues.

Before I got married, my fiancé did not want to do any pre-marital counseling. My Pastor said to me that there would be a price to pay. This was a warning for me, out of love. We moved to Washington State to raise a family. At least, that was his reasoning because we both had no family there. This was a journey I was not prepared for because of the warning I received and the directive I was given to study, hear, listen, and do.

I became a very restless person, wondering what I just did. I found myself in the middle of good versus evil, knowing that lukewarm was not an option. Getting a job was no issue for me; it was for him. He eventually got a job working nights, and I worked during the day. Our son was born a year later, who is my joy outside of God. The pleasure my son gave me was like nothing I had known, so I stayed home to raise him for the first 3.5 years.

It was rough because I was the primary income earner, so we managed the triplex we were in to keep the rent down. The bills were piling up, so I went back to work. This time, I decided to go behind the scenes and work with medical insurance companies. On my first attempt in the job market, I was hired on the spot and later became a supervisor with more responsibility. I enjoyed it very much.

I came home one day, months later, and my son and his father were not there. I called the daycare and was informed that this has been common and that my son was often left here after hours. I felt my heart was about to leave my body. I was not driving, so I used public transportation everywhere. I went to pick him up, and the lady said your son has a very high IQ. Have you thought about putting him in school? Remember, I spent quality time pouring into him. I taught him phonics, letters, reading, and writing. At age four, he was set only to get better.

I took the next few days off from work, and my husband never returned home. He called and asked me to call his job and say he would be late. I had no clue what was going on. I kept hearing my Pastor's words repeatedly, "There would be a price to pay." I returned to focusing on my son so I could get back to work. I contacted the school, and they said having someone that young in preschool is very unusual. They had to be potty trained, follow instructions, and know the alphabet. I said that is not a problem. My son can read and write. He likes to teach other kids, and seeing my child teach phonics is hilarious. It's rewarding, at least for me. Every parent can impart to their children, no matter what time you have to offer. The look on his face was priceless. I had my son with me, and he asked him his name. My son told him with such boldness and shook his hand. The man asked my son, can you spell your name? He said, "Of course, sir, I can even spell your name." The man laughed, so I asked him what his first name was. Next, I asked my son to spell the man's name, and he did! The school official was so intrigued. My son was allowed to enroll in an all-white school full-time at four years old. He was allowed to skip a grade the following year because of his advancement.

My husband came home with a strange smell on his body. He told me he thought he had a drug problem. I worked for a medical insurance company and knew all the rehab facilities. After the shock, and I mean shock, I called to get him in ASAP. I called my church, spoke to my Pastor, and explained what happened. Since I am in leadership, my Pastor told me I did the right thing. But your husband must be willing to go through the process of healing. I don't even drink, and I don't particularly appreciate taking Tylenol. How and who is he hanging around with that has this drug-addicted lifestyle?

While we had no family here in Washington State, he had friends he knew from the military and liked to get high. I wanted to meet these people. My heart got so heavy that I could only cry. I do not allow alcohol or smoking in my house. I went to work one day with such a perplexed look that one of my staff asked if I was okay. She said it's drugs. I held my head down in shame, and she said, it's not your fault. She said the times you had to leave to get your son and the phone calls; she knew it was something that you were in shock over.

Weeks later, one Sunday after church, I needed my husband to take me to get a car. He didn't mind because he just relapsed and was willing to do anything. I got to the dealership and said I wanted to buy a car, and my husband said you don't know how to drive. I said this is what God wants me to do. He stood back and watched. I told the dealer I would need financing. He took my personal information, and I was approved to purchase my car. I said I would be here on Tuesday to pick up the car.

On Monday, I went to the DMV and said I needed a driver's license and what to do. The state examiner told me I usually needed an appointment and must pass the written and driving tests. My husband was watching all this and wondering how this would turn out. I took the written test and did not pass. The man said let's do this again. He gave me an area of concern and a scenario, and I said okay, I got it. I retook the test and passed it, then I said, what's next? He said the driving test, and I said okay. I was trembling with fear. I said, okay, God, I need your supernatural strength to get through this. The man said to come back in an hour. I scheduled your road test.

I told my husband you have less than an hour to show me how to drive and parallel park. We went to an empty parking lot so I could get used to being behind the wheel. Boy, was I nervous. We went back, and I observed someone completing their test by doing hand signals. I asked my husband what that was, and he explained it (to me). I was so grateful to see this because that was the first thing the man asked me. Then, the examiner asked me to use the directional signals and adjust the mirrors. When it was time to parallel park, I was so nervous. We passed a spot with about three parking spaces, and I could park.

All I can say is thank you, God. In less than 48 hours, I got to see God move in a mighty way for me. I got 100% financing with no money down, got my license, and passed my test. I had never seen my husband so quiet, so I asked him to pick up the car for me on Tuesday. I could not because I needed to practice driving. Within two weeks, I was driving and had never been on the freeway. What a scary feeling, but I made it. I had no idea why the urgency, but God knew.

A month later, my husband entered the door on a Sunday afternoon, and my heart was beating heavily. I could not stand for long until I felt a presence holding me. In the hallway where I met him, he told me he was in a fight and a man died. He smelled so bad; all I could do was ask him to shower and freshen up. I took my son and went straight to church. I have no clue how I got there with this so heavy on my mind.

I saw my Pastor, and he asked if I was okay. I said no, and he said there was a reason he came to the church this early, but he was unsure why. I let him know that my husband had just told me he killed someone in a fight. He asked if drugs were involved, and I said I think so. He asked me to have him call first thing in the morning, and he did. He turned himself in after

I told him running would burden us and I couldn't handle that. He went to trial, was found guilty, and sentenced to fourteen years in prison.

When life calls, and life happens, God sustains and keeps you through the storms.

The next chapter begins the story of the essence of the pearl; you don't want to miss it.

About The Author

Verlin White

Verlin White was born and raised in Detroit, Michigan, in a large (family) home with loving siblings and parents. At a young age, she was called to nations for the voiceless, and through her journeys, she was trained and developed to where she is now. She has dedicated her life to teaching people the importance of understanding their values.

The cry on the inside has a voice—who will go for us?

She is a Pastor passionate about deliverance and wants to help set the captives (free) whom the son has already set free.

Verlin is a mother, a certified life coach, and an entrepreneur. One of her passions is Pearls. She specializes in helping you discover the essence of the hidden pearl, uncover your talents, and increase your value as the pearl you were created to be. She desires to help make every encounter with her a peaceful, uplifting, educational, and impactful experience.

14

Harness The Power Of Transformation

Michael Bart Mathews

My Childhood Story

As I reflect on my childhood, growing up in the 1960s and '70s, we had access to everything: good, bad, right, and wrong, we had access. To survive, earning your Doctorate Degree in Streetology from the University of Hard Knocks was a must-have. Surviving in Chicago during my childhood, adolescence, and adult life has yielded multiple traumatic blasts from my past. From running policies (the neighborhood lottery) and selling dinners to selling drugs. You could get what you wanted. Chicago bolstered some of the biggest gangs in America, and as sure as I am writing this chapter, back in the day, we could not escape gang activity. My neighborhood never joined the gangs, thanks to the older community members who protected us and kept the gangs at bay.

We traveled through gang territory to and from high school. Some of us faced bullying and public ridicule because they were unpopular or not in the 'In crowd.' Our parents had no idea about the level of stress, trauma, disruption, and uncertainty we faced daily outside of our community. They were too busy paying the bills, keeping clothes on our backs, and food on the table. I did not want to bother them with my issues Streetology issues.

On the business side, Black-owned businesses were throughout my neighborhood. If my memory serves me correctly, within a five-minute radius of my house, community resources included three churches, four corner stores, two cleaners, one fire department, three elementary schools, one concrete outdoor basketball court, one tavern, and two tool factories.

Notable residents from my community (Grand Crossing) were:

1. Gwendolyn Brooks (7428 S. Evans 1953 to 1994) – Poet, author, teacher, and recipient of the 1950 Pulitzer Prize for Poetry.
2. Gary Comer – Businessman & philanthropist, built a multi-million-dollar Comer Community Center located on 72nd and South Chicago.
3. Shani Davis – First African American to win a Gold Medal in an individual event at the Olympic Winter Games.
4. Wilton Daniel Gregory (217 W. 72nd Street) – the first African American Cardinal.
5. Michelle Obama & Craig Robinson – (6330-6546 S. King Drive) Lived in Parkway Gardens Apartments at a young age before the family moved to South Shore.
6. Michael Bart Mathews (72nd University/Woodlawn) – Athlete, Poet, Writer, Author, Speaker, Entrepreneur.

The authority figures growing up in an all-Black neighborhood (outside of the adults in my community) were white. The police officers, firefighters, schoolteachers, news reporters, insurance men, delivery drivers, City Transit Bus Operators, Doctors, and Nurses were all white. Yes, I saw a few Black teachers, and all the Preachers Were Black; however, without any discriminatory intent, outside of the Black Business Owners, white men held the positions of authority. Sometimes, that authority caused traumatic experiences because they felt empowered to say things and do things that were derogatory in the eyes of my young mind. Those early experiences taught me to keep my eyes open, listen, learn, and begin to understand how to navigate the game of life.

My Mother and Auntie left the South in their early teens by catching a Greyhound Bus during the great migration North to Chicago. They told me stories filled with trauma-related issues that I never forgot about, including my Mom's experience with picking cotton in the hot sun all day, every day as a child. I knew my Grandpa and Grandma on my mother's side; however, I only knew my Grandma on my father's side. I remember the stories about my Grandpa on my father's side that were passed down to me from my father and my cousins.

My father and my uncles were subjected to Jim Crow dictatorship while growing up in the South, which caused my father to join the great migration North across the Mason-Dixion Line in his early twenties. My father and mother met later and married, having three children, with me being the youngest.

<u>Back to the Story:</u>

We took road trips every summer during my childhood. My father packed the car, and my mother fried a basket of chicken, bread, cakes, cookies, chips, and water. Off we went down South to visit my mother's and father's side of the family.

We stopped for gas after crossing into Effingham, Illinois, a Sundown town. A sundown town was a white community that excluded Blacks using intimidation, violence, and discriminatory laws. Remember, we were born and raised (up North) in Chicago and had never been exposed to white-only and colored-only public restrooms. My older sister ran out of the car and raced toward the white-only restroom. Four to five white men were sitting in front of the gas station, openly carrying shotguns and rifles. They stood up before my sister could touch the doorknob of the white-only restroom; my mother grabbed her and stopped her in her tracks.

The white men sat down as my mother and sister hurried to use the color-only restroom. My father was watching as he continued pumping gas. Afterward, he took my brother and me to the colored-only restroom after paying for the gas, and we drove off with no incident.

As we continued our journey deeper into the South, my parents gave us a verbal lesson on racism, segregation, and discrimination, which included our recent traumatic experience back at the gas station.

My Adolescent Story:

As I reflect on my adolescent years, between the ages of 12 and 18, I was not mature enough to listen to my inner guiding system, that man who sits on your shoulder and suggests that you do or don't do this or that. Some call it intuition, sixth sense,' or simply acting upon your feelings.

Allow me to take you on a journey that leads to a moment in time that will forever be with me.

I was a high school student-athlete, playing on the varsity basketball team as the starting center. I was around 16 years old, and I had a wonderful girlfriend. I'll call her Mickey. I was good friends with Mickey's cousin, who attended high school with me. One day, Mickey came to visit her cousin, and we met. From then on, it was Mickey and me, hand in hand.

Mickey would visit her cousin, and that's where we would meet. We would do things teenagers did. Mickey lived in the Chicago Housing Projects. I'm not knocking the families and some of my friends who lived in the projects; I'm simply highlighting that if you did not live in the projects and came to visit someone, everyone knew you didn't belong. That was the case with me.

Our basketball team was a contender for the Illinois Class A.A. Boys High School State Basketball Championship. Mickey would occasionally tell me that her mother wanted to meet me. Remember, Mickey's family lived in the projects; I had never been in her building. Whenever Mickey asked me to meet her mother, I felt uncomfortable inside. My inner guiding system made me feel uneasy about making the trip. It was not about FEAR; it was about having enough Streetology to know where and where not to go. Remember, Chicago had several of the largest gangs of any city in America.

On that fateful day, Mickey asked me (again) to meet her mother. Mickey would show her mother newspaper clippings of our winning basketball team. Her mother wanted to meet me to gauge our intentions.

It was time for our team to play in the City of Chicago, Class A.A. High School Basketball City Championship Game. The newspapers, radio, and television stations covered the game big time, and Mickey continued sharing our basketball success with her mother. Against my feelings from my inner guiding system, institution, and Streetology, I decided it would not hurt to make one visit, meet Mickey's Mother and family, and leave quietly.

I asked my father if I could drive his car, and for the first time during my high school days, my Dad said yes. Mickey and I went to visit her family, especially her mother. We arrived at her building (The Robert Taylor Chicago Public Housing Projects) on State Street in Chicago, parked, and entered the building. About eight to ten youngsters stood out front as we approached the elevators. They all said hello, Mickey. I felt better because I thought these were her friends. They did not verbally speak to me. However, they gave me the customary head nod, and I returned (the nod) without saying a word.

We rode the elevator to the 16th floor, which stopped on every floor. Every time the door opened, I got strange looks from the people getting on and off. They knew I did live there. They all knew and spoke to Mickey, so for the second time, I felt we would be okay. We got off the elevator. Mickey used her key to open the door, and her mother sat on the couch with a big smile. She stands up, walks over to me, gives me a long, tight hug, and says, it's so lovely to meet you.

Her family comes out, we exchange pleasantries, and the Good-Times begin over a home-cooked meal. Florida & Thelma Evans could not have cooked a better meal! By now, my inhibitions of uncomfortable feelings were completely gone. Mickey's family welcomed me with open arms.

It was getting late, and I had to have my Dad's car back at a specific time, and I did not want to mess up. We said goodbyes, rode the elevator to the ground floor and exited the building. Unbeknownst to me, the guys in front of the building, who had spoken to Mickey when we came in, were still there, as if they were waiting for us to leave.

Without warning, several of the guys pulled out guns, and one of the guys put a gun up to my head, cocked the trigger, and told me not to move. I still remember hearing the sound from the tumbler when he pulled the trigger. They told Mickey she better not say anything as he went through my pockets. We better not call the police. Don't forget, Mickey, your family lives in this building, and you do not want anything to happen to them, do you? They took the little money I had in my pockets and my Dad's car keys. They took Mickey's purse, and one of the guys emptied it and took what little money she had. Remember, the robbers called Mickey by name because they lived in the same building.

I asked them if I could have my Dad's car keys back. One of the guys threw the keys and hit me in the chest. I could feel the pain because my Dad had a large ring full of keys. I was worried about Mickey and me the entire time, but there was nothing I could do. The robbers looked like elementary school-age children, and they all had handguns. This was happening in broad daylight!

Suddenly, a guardian angel appeared out of nowhere. An older man (a stranger) saw what was happening and began shooting up in the air to scare the robbers away. Unfortunately, as the robbers ran away, they turned around and shot at me and Mickey. I could hear bullets bouncing off the brick building. I saw sparks flying upon impact. Writing this narrative reminded me of how I pushed Mickey to the ground, trying to escape harm's way. I did not think; I reacted based on instinct.

After the robbers were gone, I noticed my girlfriend, Mickey, had been shot. I was out of my mind. Blood was everywhere, Mickey was crying, she was in pain, and I was in a strange neighborhood. The Guardian Angel (That older man) helped me put Mickey into the back seat of my Dad's car. He told me to drive her to Provident Hospital on 51st. On the way to the hospital, Mickey was still crying from the pain. I was nervous and sped until I arrived at the emergency room. I shouted to a couple of hospital personnel wearing scrubs that my girlfriend had been shot and needed medical attention. They took her out of the back seat, put her on a gurney, and rushed her into the emergency room after examining her wound. I did not know if Mickey was going to live or die. I nervously walked up and down the hallway, not knowing what else to do. I was all alone, 16 years old.

While at the hospital, the doctors took care of Mickey's wound. Thank God it was not life-threatening. The doctors came out and gave me the good news. Two detectives showed up at the hospital and told us we had to come down to the police station to look at mug shots and try to identify the gunmen.

Mickey begged me not to point them out, even if I recognized them, because of the threat of harm the robbers promised to inflict on her family. While looking at the mugshots, I can honestly say that I did not recognize them. I do not know what I would have done if I had. Because of the trauma of getting a gun pointed at my head, hearing the sound of the trigger being cocked, getting robbed, shot at, and my girlfriend getting shot, my mind, body, spirit, and soul were off balance.

Even though I was an adolescent, my inner child went into fear mode because I did not understand what just happened. My adolescent self went into flight mode of survival. I did not have time to freeze, and I had nothing to fight back with because I did not carry a gun. Had I been carrying a gun, I might have shot back and changed the trajectory of my young life that I could not undo. I chose flight because it was my best option to get Mickey to the hospital as soon as possible. At that point, I thought about Mickey's health and safety.

At age 16, I could not have explained this to you calmly. However, because today, I am a Certified Addiction Recovery Coach with Trauma-related training, I looked back into my life to understand the effect that trauma had on me. As you continue reading my story, if you are suffering in silence from a trauma-related past or present experience, there is help for you. You are not alone.

Now, back to my story!

Mickey called her mother from the pay phone. Back in the day, a local public telephone call from a phone booth cost 10 cents. Her family met us at the police station and took her home.

I was nervously driving home, still in disbelief, shock, and traumatized over what had just happened. I had not experienced being trauma-informed, so I played the hand I had just been dealt. It was well past when I was supposed to have my Dad's car back, and I did not know what kind of mood he would be in. I explained the situation, and all was forgiven.

After all that took place, we went on to win the Chicago City Basketball Championship, and we headed downstate with my High School basketball team and student body to play in the Illinois High School Basketball State Tournament. During the tournament, our basketball team members were called different racial slurs, including ghetto dwellers. Because we were well-coached and understood what was at stake, we steadied our course on the road to the championship. We eventually won to become the 1973 Illinois High School Basketball State Champion. After graduating from high school, Mickey and I enjoyed the summer, and I went off to college in the fall.

My Young Adult Story

During my third semester in college, I received a call or letter (I don't remember which one) from Mickey's cousin. She told me that Mickey had been killed in a head-on car collision on a two-lane highway alone with Mickey's cousin. The highway patrol report stated they both were D.O.I., dead on impact. I could not imagine the amount of pain and suffering they endured until taking their last breath.

Mickey's death was my second trauma-related experience with my girlfriend. My latest experience with trauma was a big deal for me because

I knew I would not physically have Mickey in my life again. Imagine this: You are 18 years old, away from family and friends, and you receive news that your girl or boyfriend has been killed. I had no grief counselor, no therapist, no spiritual advisor, no nothing to help me cope with this latest tragedy. Memories of Mickey and I getting shot at and Mickey getting shot resurfaced at the forefront of my thoughts. My college classmates knew nothing about what I went through with Mickey. I put it all behind me and out of my mind, or so I thought! The news of Mickey's death triggered our past shared trauma experience once again. Now, I was dealing with unresolved past trauma, on top of adding another trauma-related experience.

I discussed my unbelievable situation with my college basketball coach, and he was afraid I would not return to school if I went home to Chicago to attend Mickey's homegoing services. He did not want me to leave for Mickey's homegoing services.

Well, that made me even more mentally upset. I called my parents, and they said all the right things. But I felt alone with my thoughts. I wanted to know why this happened to Mickey and me after we had just overcome being robbed and shot at. I honestly do not remember if I reached out to my Higher Power during this time. I don't remember saying a prayer. As I looked back in time, I knew God was with me.

One of my friends (we are still friends today) loaned me his car, which had a full tank of gas, and off I went back to Chicago to attend Mickey's funeral. I saw her cousin, Mother, and other family members. After the services, I rested at my parents' house before returning to college. I had already made up my mind that I was going to leave because I felt the coach cared more about my basketball ability than he did about my mental health during my time of need.

Was this a good, bad, right, or wrong decision? I knew I had to make it because my inner guiding system no longer felt comfortable with this coach's lack of remorse, compassion, and leadership, especially when I needed it outside of playing basketball. Remember, I was 18 years old. Making that decision changed my life.

What if my college basketball coach was trauma-informed and understood trauma-related issues? What if my basketball coach had suggested that I speak with a therapist, psychologist, or spiritual counselor (Pastor/Preacher/Reverend)? I might have dealt with the situation differently! Let's move forward.

My dear readers, if you need help finding your moment of clarity, seek help. Do not suffer in silence. The coauthors of this amazing book, "My Life My Story," share our stories because we want you to know that you are not alone. The glory in our stories is designed to be an illuminating light on your pathway to trauma recovery. No, we are not living in our past. However, we are opening up the transformation story that empowers us to Be, Do, and Have ***Limitless*** potential because we are ***Inspired2Speak*** about our experiences.

After leaving college, I felt empty and lost and had no real plan. I began drinking and smoking marijuana like Cheech & Chong in the movie, 'Up In Smoke". I started hanging out in toxic places and doing harmful things with toxic people. None of that mattered at that time. As I look back, I was trying to cope with my post-trauma-related experiences with Mickey, and the solution was alcohol and drugs. From there, I started using cocaine.

I started playing basketball in the summer, trying to return to normal. However, thoughts of losing Mickey to a car accident were ever present all the time. I began having mental obsessions about not being able to be with Mickey, in the flesh, in my arms. She was no longer physically present to cheer me on at my basketball games. The more I became mentally obsessed over the death of Mickey, the more I began to spiral deeper and deeper into alcohol and drugs.

I had a spiritual awakening one morning, and I stopped drinking and drugging and cleaned myself up without any outside intervention. No A.A., Alcoholics Anonymous; at that point in my life, I had not heard of

Alcoholics Anonymous, Detox Treatment Centers, The 12-Step Program, a Sponsor, or Halfway Houses. I knew my awakening had to be spiritual because the earthly, human side of me was ready, willing, and able to get as high as a kite and land on cloud nine. But I stopped because of divine intervention after speaking my sinner prayer into existence! But this part of my story continues down the road.

I transferred to another college, played basketball, and got back in order.

My Adult Story

After college, I returned to the same toxic people and places and started doing the same toxic things (alcohol, marijuana, and cocaine). I knew where to score drugs, and it was as easy as buying a gallon of milk. I tried my hand at drug dealing, and I did not like the fact that the cell phone rang every two or three minutes, every day, all day long! There were all levels of people, from Main Street to Wall Street, who were scoring drugs—white collar corporate professionals, politicians, doctors, lawyers, law enforcement, firefighters, professional athletes, dentists, husbands, wives, working single mothers, and your everyday man or woman.

Looking back on those days, I didn't do it for the money. I did it because it looked cool and took my mind off Mickey. I met many interesting people. I was living the nightlife during my transitional period from working in nightclubs.

During the day, I worked a full-time job. No one at my day job knew about my nightlife, which was fantastic. I was Dr. Jekyll (a well-respected, intelligent person) during the day. And Mr. Hyde (the darker side of my existence) at night. In other words, I was living a double life. However, I did accept responsibility for my good, bad, right, and wrong actions from my self-determination.

I had phenomenal cravings during the day, but I never drank or used drugs during working hours. I was always walking on pins and needles because our company had a mandatory random drug testing policy. Once again, my Higher Power watched over me. I did not take a drug test. The level of drugs in my system was enough to register me out of employment. I never considered myself to be an alcoholic or addicted. I know the A.A. 12-step program would say differently. However, I believe that what we confess, we possess – Earl Nightengale. I could accept that I abused alcohol and drugs, but I was not addicted. I did not know what addiction was back then, so I never bought into that terminology.

One morning, after a night of getting high, I came to work, and my eyes were red as a delicious apple. My coworker asked me if there was something wrong with me. I said I was off my square. My coworker thought nothing of it because I never missed a workday. I took an FMLA-Family Medical Leave Act day off, went home, and started getting high. I had a shoebox full of White China cocaine at my disposal. More mental obsessions kicked in, and I was paranoid that if I went back to work and had to take a drug test, I would fail and lose my job. My phenomenal cravings grew stronger and stronger. It got so bad or good that I called in to work and took two weeks of FMLA days off. During those two weeks, I occasionally got high.

My question for you, my dear readers: Have you ever experienced what seemed to be a miracle (Blessing) during a dark moment in your life?

Here's my miracle, or shall I say, Blessing! I woke up one morning (the second and final time) and said enough is enough of getting high. My Higher Power came and changed my life forever. Once again, for the second time, I recited my sinner's prayer to my Higher Power. Here are my exact words: Quote: "God, I know I am a sinner. I know I am going to commit other sins because I am human. If you take this sin away from me, I will never do this sin again." My prayer was intentional. I went to sleep, and my phenomenal craving for drugs and alcohol no longer existed when I woke up the next day. I put the remaining half shoebox full of cocaine underneath my bed and forgot about it. I went back to work with the 100-pound monkey off my back. I was now feeling excited and ready. No mental obsessions, no withdrawals, no shaking, no detox treatment, no halfway house, no AA-12 Step Program, no nothing, O.M.G.! The exception was my Higher Power! I asked, and my transformation was given to me! I knocked, and the door of cleanliness was given to me. I was seeking, and I found a responsible way of living.

Six months had gone by, and my mind was not on getting high. While looking for one of my shoes under my bed, I unexpectedly found the shoebox full of cocaine. Guess what? My first thought was to start getting high again. My phenomenal craving returned because I was holding a toxic drug (cocaine) in my hands once again. My self-determination was not to spiral back down that destructive path of drinking and drugging, and I made the decision not to drink or use.

My next thought was to go back around the dope houses and sell my half shoebox of cocaine. The street value was worth thousands of dollars. Once again, my self-determination kicked in. I decided against selling drugs because I could not do the time, so I did not do the crime. Finally, I decided to flush the cocaine down the toilet and move on with my life. Why? Remember, I recited my sinner's prayer to my Higher Power. Quote: "God, I know I am a sinner. I know I am going to commit other sins because I am human. If you take this sin away from me, I will never do this sin again.

I was very intentional with what I needed my Higher Power to do. Now, here's the kicker: I never got drug tested at work, I never lost a job, I never got arrested for possession of illegal substances, I never entered into a detox alcohol and drug rehabilitation treatment center, I never stayed in a halfway house, I never followed the A.A., 12-step program, I never attended any meetings, and I never had a sponsor. I was fully functional, maintaining the highest level of workplace performance because I did understand that the consequences of my action (of discovery) could cost me everything in the blink of an eye. I did see my life flash before me, and what I saw was rock bottom with a broken foundation if I did not change my pattern of living. To this day, I have not used any illegal drugs since that faithful day I recited my sinner's prayer to my Higher Power over 40+ years ago. This part of my life was before I met my wife. I met my wife, Robbie S. Mathews (Vice President of a Fortune 500 Financial Services Institution), and we put together a plan of action for success.

Yes, I shared my past with her because I did not want anyone pulling my skeletons out of my closet for their personal gain. It was my story, and I told it with an unapologetic, fearless, shameless attitude. Why? Because that was not who I was when I met Robbie. I wanted to be open and honest and let the chips fall where they may! I wanted to give Robbie the opportunity to love me for who I am, not who I once was.

Making a positive PARADIGM SHIFT (fundamental change using self-determination) is just a decision away! Graduating from the School of Hard Knocks and The University of Lifeology is possible. We must remember, "Every Day Is a Life-Long Learning Process," what we live, we learn! My Life, My Story!

About The Author

Michael Bart Mathews

Michael "Bart" Mathews is a successful International Speaker, #1 New Book Release Award-Winning Author, Entrepreneur, and Investor. Michael and Robbie have been on the same stage (or seated in the audience) with international figureheads worldwide. Such notables as Al Pacino- "The Godfather," John Travolta, 50 Cent-Rapper/Actor, Mark Walberg/Christie Brinkley-Sports Illustrated Cover Girl Super Model/Business Mogul, Bethany Frankel-Founder of Skinny Girl Wine/Calvin Klein-Fashion Designer/Fredrik Eklund-Bravo Television Million Dollar Listing New York/Randi Zuckerberg-former Director of Market Development at Facebook/Mike Ditka 1985 Chicago Bears N.F.L. Super Bowl Champions/ Nelson Mandela's grandson; Nadba Mandela/Kofi Annan-Former Secretary General & joint Noble Peace Prize winner (2001) with the United Nations/Dr. Ervin Laszlo, twice nominated for the Noble Peace Prize in 2004-05/Mirela Sula-Global Woman Magazine Founder/Dr. Sonja Stribling, Former Bravo TV

Host/Les Brown, Baron Sir Dr. James Dentley and Baroness Dr. Kara Dentley/Jack Canfield, Mark Victor Hanson/Matthew McCaughey/Demi Moore/Wesley Snipes, and Ashton Kutcher.

In February 2017, Michael and Robbie shared their international presentation in the beautiful country of South Africa. Together, they spoke to around 1,200 attendees from 21 countries. Randi Zuckerberg and Nelson Mandela's grandson, Ndaba Mandela, were also speaking. Robbie interviewed Ndaba Mandela.

On May 10, 2017, Michael and Robbie attended retired N.F.L. Marques Odgen's Speaker Academy with other N.F.L. players, Walt Harris, Justin C. Smith, Kyle Bradey, Donte Jones, and other professionals.

On July 15, 2017, Michael and Robbie shared the stage with more talented people. High-profile personalities like Suzanne Le` Mignot-CBS Channel 2 News Journalist, D. Channsin Berry-Film Producer, and Cynda Williams-Actress (Spike Lee). Others included Tony Grant-Singer/Actor (Tyler Perry) and event organizer Quinton de` Alexander at the "We Dream in Color Humanitarian Celebration." In addition, Michael received the Businessman of the Year award, named after John H. Johnson, founder of Ebony & Jet Magazine, in honor of his humanitarian efforts to help make this world better.

On Sunday, June 23, 2024, Mike/Robbie received the Difference Maker Award from JD3TV, Inspired2Speak & Limitless from the Dentleys.

Michael's literary journey has afforded him the privilege of working with 200+ writers in 17 countries, resulting in 90+ published authors and many successful writers in other literary capacities.

They are Advisory Board Members of the Always Already Amazing Charitable Foundation, started by their dear friends, Baron Sir Dr. James III and Baroness Dr. Kara Dentley, in the Chicagoland Area. They are also Benefactors of the Monarchical Chapter of the Sovereign and Royal House of Cappadocia.

Contact Michael Bart Mathews:

Email: wecreatebooks@tmeginc.com
Linktr.ee: https://Linktr.ee/michaelbartmathews
Facebook: https://www.facebook.com/michaelbartmathews
LinkedIn: https://www.linkedin.com/in/michaelbartmathews
Limitless TV: https://jd3tv.com/michael-bart-mathews

Or call him at: +1 (708) 634 6787

Get Your Free Gift at https://www.tmeginc.com/specialgift

Made in the USA
Columbia, SC
03 June 2025

58861343R00109